Learner-Mana
and Home Education:
A European Perspective

Apprentissage auto-géré
et instruction à la maison:
une perspective européenne

Selbstbestimmtes Lernen
und Bildung ohne Schule:
eine europäische Perspektive

Editor / Sous la direction de / Herausgeber
Leslie Safran Barson

Foreword by Dr. Robert Bell
European Forum for Freedom in Education (EFFE)

Avant-propos du Dr Robert Bell
Forum européen pour la liberté en éducation (EFFE)

Vorwort von Dr. Robert Bell
Europäisches Forum für Freiheit im Bildungswesen (EFFE)

Published 2006 by Educational Heretics Press
113 Arundel Drive, Bramcote, Nottingham NG9 3FQ
Copyright © 2006 Learning Unlimited

British Cataloguing in Publication Data

Barson, Leslie (ed)
　　　　Learner-managed Learning and Home Education:
　　　　A European Perspective.

A catalogue reference for this volume is available from the British Library

ISBN: 1900219 31 X

Cover design by Frederic Fandard

Design and production: Learning Unlimited with Educational Heretics Press

Printed by Mastaprint Plus, Sandiacre, Nottingham NG10 5AH

Dedication

We would like to dedicate this book to Janet and Roland Meighan and Educational Heretics Press in grateful appreciation for their total commitment to home education over many years. Their continued support, wisdom and determination have become part of the foundation of home education in the UK and beyond.

Dédicace

Nous souhaitons dédier ce livre à Janet et Roland Meighan et à Educational Heretics Press, en les remerciant vivement pour leur engagement total envers l'instruction à la maison depuis de nombreuses d'années. Leur soutien, détermination et sagesse ont contribué fondamentalement à l'instruction à la maison au Royaume Uni et au-delà de ses frontières.

Widmung

Wir widmen dieses Buch Janet und Roland Meighan und der 'Educational Heretics Press', in dankbarer Anerkennung ihres einzigartigen und langjährigen Engagements für die Belange einer Bildung ohne Schulbesuch und in Familieninitiative. Ihre anhaltende Unterstützung, ihre Weisheit und ihre Entschlossenheit trugen dazu bei, für die 'Bildung zuhause' in Großbritannien und darüber hinaus den Grundstein zu legen.

Acknowledgements

There are so many people to thank without whom this publication would never have come to fruition: Jennifer Fandard, Andy Blewett, Hes Fes and the Hes Fes Crew, the translators at Hes Fes, Janie Spencer, Roselyne Jacquemart and Alex Pletscher; Frédéric Fandard for the cover design; translators and proof readers covering the three different languages which are spoken in the different countries: in the UK, Carrie and Alex Pletscher, Barbara Stark, Dr Kem Thompson, Andrea Granville; in France, Agnès Ohlenbusch, Anne Evans, Brigitte Guimbal, Jennifer Fandard, Janie Spencer, Isabelle Guilbert Mellan, Charlotte Toscani, Frederique Bianchi, Christelle Bachelet, Martine Temple; in Germany, Matthias Kern, Elisabeth Kuhnle, Gisela Moukam, Rosa-Rosea Mousaliotis, Petra Schweitzer, Angelika Seifriz; and in Switzerland, Coni Lagler.

Remerciements

Il y a beaucoup de personnes à remercier, sans qui cette publication n'aurait jamais vu le jour : Jennifer Fandard ; Andy Blewett, organisateur de Hes Fes et l'équipe de Hes Fes ; les traducteurs à Hes Fes : Janie Spencer, Roselyne Jacquemart et Alex Pletscher ; Frédéric Fandard pour la couverture ; les traducteurs et relecteurs couvrant les trois langues parlées dans les différents pays :
- au Royaume Uni : Carrie et Alex Pletscher, Barbara Stark, Dr Kem Thompson, Andrea Granville,
- en France : Agnès Ohlenbusch, Anne Evans, Brigitte Guimbal, Jennifer Fandard, Janie Spencer, Isabelle Guilbert Mellan, Charlotte Toscani, Frédérique Bianchi, Christelle Bachelet, Martine Temple,
- en Allemagne : Matthias Kern, Elisabeth Kunhle, Gisela Moukam, Rosa-Rosea Mousaliotis, Petra Schweitzer, Angelika Seifriz
- et en Suisse : Coni Lagler.

Danksagung

Es gebührt vielen Menschen Dank, ohne die dieses Buch niemals verwirklicht worden wäre: Andy Blewett, 'Hes Fes', und der 'Hes Fes Crew' und Jennifer Fandard; den Übersetzern auf dem Hes Fes, Janie Spencer, Roselyne Jacquemart und Alex Pletscher; Frédéric Fandard für die Einbandgestaltung. Den Übersetzern und Korrekturlesern, welche die Texte in den drei verschiedenen Sprachen – Englisch, Französisch, Deutsch – bearbeitet haben, die in den vier verschiedenen Ländern gesprochen werden. In Großbritannien: Carrie und Alex Pletscher, Barbara Stark, Dr. Kem Thompson; in Frankreich: Agnès Ohlenbusch, Anne Evans, Brigitte Guimbal, Jennifer Fandard, Janie Spencer, Isabelle Guilbert Mellan, Charlotte Toscani, Frédérique Bianchi, Chistelle Bachelet und Korrekturleserin Martine Temple; in Deutschland: Matthias Kern, Elisabeth Kunhle, Stefanie Mohsennia, Gisela Moukam, Rosa-Rosea Mousaliotis, Petra Schweitzer, Angelika Seifriz; und in der Schweiz: Coni Lagler.

Contents/ Sommaire/ Inhalt

Part II

Foreword

by Dr. Robert Bell
Vice President, European Forum for Freedom in Education(EFFE)

Anyone who attended last summer's gathering of British home educators at Hes Fes (Home Educators' Seaside Festival) could have no doubt about the enthusiasm and confidence of the home education movement or could believe that the parents involved had not thought carefully about their decision to keep their children out of school. Yet the vast majority of people in Europe still have grave doubts about home education and while they accept that such an arrangement may be necessary in the Australian outback or on remote Scottish islands, the idea of deliberately keeping children away from a readily available school seems to show a perverse, or even reckless disregard for those children's welfare. All too often they see home education simply as an inferior form of schooling with arrogant, untrained parents doing what is clearly a teacher's job in an amateurish, inefficient manner.

But what is most striking about the articles in this collection is the overwhelmingly affirmative nature of the decision made by those parents wishing to educate at home. They may wish to avoid schools, of course, seeing them as restricting, authoritarian places but most home educators nowadays are thinking far more positively in terms of the actual educational advantages of non-schooling. They relish the liberating effects of freeing children from the strict injunctions of a common timetable to pursue their own learning instincts that have already enabled them to embrace successfully so many skills including the complex task of learning their own language. They are also realistic about what learning is possible in a single home. The networks of families that are being created and the use that is being made of communal facilities extends the educational arena way beyond what parents can stimulate or facilitate on their own or what schools could provide even with enlarged budgets. Such adventures provide new scope for social interaction as well as for the autonomous learning on the part of the child that can sometimes make redundant any formal teaching whether by inexperienced parents or trained teachers.

i

The articles here by Roland Meighan and Alan Thomas recall the cogent de-schooling arguments of the 1970s that were really beginning to influence educational thinking in England but were stopped in their tracks by the sudden appearance of the juggernaut National Curriculum with all its institutional assumptions. Meighan provides a timely reminder that primary and secondary schools are just two in a whole range of teaching/learning agents available to the children of the 21st century while Thomas highlights the informal learning that is taking place all around us and can prove far more effective and lasting in its impact than conventional schooling.

The sad thing is, of course, that in many parts of Europe, parents are still not free to reject such schooling, This is especially true in Germany, and even where it is legally possible, as in Britain and France, home education is all too often under constant suspicion and subject to rigorous inspection on very traditional and largely inappropriate lines. My own organisation, the European Forum for Freedom in Education (EFFE) takes seriously any attempts by governments to limit the right of parents to decide the nature of their child's education. Such a right is guaranteed in declarations of both the Council of Europe and the United Nations adopted by virtually all European governments. Those who forbid home schooling are not just breaking their own promise to respect parents' wishes, they are also now impeding educational experiments that could have favourable consequences for the whole of our society. Let's hope it won't be too long before the truth dawns.

Avant-propos

par Dr Robert Bell

Vice Président du Forum Européen pour la Liberté en Education (EFFE)

Quiconque a participé l'été dernier à la rencontre d'Hes Fes (Home Educators' Seaside Festival) des familles britanniques instruisant leurs enfants à domicile, ne pourrait avoir aucun doute quant à l'enthousiasme et la confiance du mouvement des familles ayant fait ce choix ni croire que ces parents ont pris à la légère une décision de ne pas envoyer leurs enfants à l'école. Pourtant, la vaste majorité des gens en Europe ont encore des doutes sérieux sur l'instruction hors école et alors qu'ils acceptent que ce genre de situation puisse être nécessaire dans l'arrière-pays d'Australie ou sur des îles reculées d'Ecosse, l'idée qu'on puisse délibérément choisir de ne pas laisser ses enfants fréquenter une école parfaitement disponible paraît comme un refus pervers ou irresponsable de veiller à leur bien-être. Trop souvent, l'instruction familiale est vue comme une forme inférieure d'éducation menée par des parents arrogants, sans formation, qui essaient de faire d'une manière maladroite et inefficace ce qui est clairement un travail d'enseignant professionnel.

En réalité, au contraire, ce qui est le plus remarquable dans ce recueil d'articles c'est à quel point la décision des parents qui choisissent l'instruction à la maison est assumée. Bien entendu, ils peuvent souhaiter éviter les écoles qu'ils considèrent comme des lieux contraignants et autoritaires, mais la plupart des familles ayant fait ce choix aujourd'hui pensent plutôt en termes positifs aux avantages que représentent, d'un point de vue éducatif, une instruction sans école. Ils sont contents de libérer leurs enfants des contraintes strictes d'un horaire scolaire afin que ceux-ci suivent leurs propres instincts en matière d'apprentissage, instincts qui leur ont déjà permis de maîtriser beaucoup de compétences, y compris d'accomplir la tâche complexe d'apprendre leur propre langue. Ces parents sont réalistes aussi quant aux possibilités restreintes d'une instruction limitée à leur domicile. La création de réseaux de familles et l'usage qui est fait d'installations communales permettent d'étendre le terrain éducatif bien au-delà de ce que les parents peuvent susciter ou faciliter eux-mêmes et de ce que les écoles peuvent offrir, même avec un budget important. De telles expériences fournissent de nouvelles occasions pour l'interaction sociale et pour un apprentissage autonome de la part de l'enfant, ce qui peut parfois rendre superflu tout enseignement formel, que ce soit par des parents inexpérimentés ou des enseignants formés.

Les articles de Roland Meighan et d'Alan Thomas rappellent les arguments pertinents sur la déscolarisation de la société des années 1970, qui commençaient à influencer la pensée en matière d'instruction en Angleterre, mais qui ont été réduits à néant par l'arrivée soudaine du programme scolaire national, rouleau compresseur avec toutes ses présomptions institutionnelles. Meighan rappelle opportunément que les écoles primaires et secondaires ne sont que deux composantes du vaste éventail des possibilités d'enseignement et d'apprentissage ouvertes aux enfants du $21^{\text{ème}}$ siècle, tandis que Thomas met en évidence l'apprentissage informel qui a lieu tout autour de nous et qui peut s'avérer beaucoup plus efficace et durable dans son impact que la scolarisation conventionnelle.

Ce qui est triste, bien sûr, est que dans plusieurs parties d'Europe, les parents n'ont pas la liberté de rejeter cette scolarisation. C'est le cas en particulier en Allemagne, et même lorsque c'est légalement possible, comme en Grande Bretagne ou en France, l'instruction à domicile fait trop souvent l'objet de suspicions constantes et d'inspections rigoureuses selon des critères très traditionnels et souvent très inappropriés. L'organisation à laquelle j'appartiens, Le Forum Européen pour la Liberté en Education (EFFE), prend très au sérieux toutes les tentatives des gouvernements de limiter le droit des parents de choisir le type d'éducation qu'ils donnent à leurs enfants. Ce droit est garanti par les déclarations du Conseil de l'Europe et des Nations Unies, adoptées par quasiment tous les gouvernements européens. Ceux qui interdisent l'instruction à domicile ne tiennent pas non seulement leur propre promesse de respecter les souhaits des parents, mais empêchent que se réalisent des expériences en éducation qui pourraient avoir des conséquences positives pour notre société entière. Espérons que la vérité ne tardera pas trop à se faire jour.

Vorwort

von Dr. Robert Bell

Vizepräsident des 'European Forum for Freedom in Education' ('Europäisches Forum für Freiheit im Bildungswesen' -EFFE)

Beim letzten Sommertreffen britischer 'home educators' (Familien mit Kindern, die sich ohne Schulbesuch bilden), dem 'Hes Fes' ('Home Educators´ Seaside Festival'), konnte niemand an der Begeisterung und der Zuversicht der Menschen aus der 'home education'-Bewegung zweifeln. Und die betroffenen Eltern hatten die Entscheidung, ihre Kinder nicht in eine Schule zu schicken, offensichtlich sorgfältig und mit Bedacht getroffen. Die überwältigende Mehrheit der Menschen in Europa hegt noch immer starke Zweifel, wenn es um die Akzeptanz von Bildungswegen ohne Schulbesuch und in Familieninitiative geht. Die Vorstellung, dass Bildung zu Hause eine im australischen 'Outback' oder auf fernen schottischen Inseln nötige Einrichtung ist, stößt zwar noch auf Verständnis, dass es aber Kinder gibt, die vorsätzlich vom Besuch einer leicht erreichbaren Schule abgehalten werden, erscheint vielen als eigensinnige oder gar rücksichtslose Missachtung des Kindeswohles. Allzu häufig wird in der privat organisierten Bildung zu Hause eine minderwertige Form der Unterrichtung gesehen, wobei arrogante und unqualifizierte Eltern in laienhafter und ineffizienter Weise übernehmen, was eindeutig die Arbeit eines professionellen Lehrers ist.

Das erstaunlichste an den Beiträgen der hier vorliegenden Sammlung ist jedoch, dass die Entscheidung jener Eltern, die ihre Kinder zu Hause lernen lassen möchten, in geradezu überwältigender Weise von einer positiven Überzeugung getragen wird. Freilich werden Schulen auch deswegen gemieden, weil Eltern sie als Orte der Einengung und Bevormundung erleben. Heutzutage jedoch hegen die meisten Eltern unbeschulter Kinder einen wesentlich positiveren Denkansatz: sie erkennen die pädagogischen Vorteile, die eine Bildung ohne Schulbesuch und ohne Unterweisung tatsächlich mit sich bringt. Sie genießen die befreienden Auswirkungen, wenn Kinder vor den starren Zwängen eines für alle gültigen Stundenplanes bewahrt werden und aus eigenem, inneren Antrieb weiterlernen können. Dieses Lernen aus ihrem eigenen, inneren Antrieb hat die Kinder ja bereits dazu befähigt, sich erfolgreich eine Vielzahl von Fertigkeiten anzueignen –

darin inbegriffen das vielschichtige Unternehmen, ihre eigene Muttersprache zu erlernen.

Sie sehen auch ganz realistisch, wie umfassend die Lernmöglichkeiten innerhalb der Familie sind – und wo diese in einem Einzelhaushalt an ihre Grenzen stoßen. Die Netzwerke, die von den Familien gebildet werden, sowie die kommunalen Einrichtungen, die gegenwärtig in Anspruch genommen werden, erweitern den Lern- und Erfahrungsraum über das hinaus, was einzelne Eltern anregen oder ermöglichen können, oder was Schulen – selbst wenn sie finanziell besser ausgestattet wären – anbieten könnten. Solche Abenteuer geben sowohl den sozialen Wechselbeziehungen als auch dem freien und selbstbestimmten Lernen der Kinder eine neue Dimension. Dadurch wird in manchen Fällen jeglicher formale Unterricht – einerlei ob nun von unerfahrenen Eltern oder von ausgebildeten Lehrern gegeben – überflüssig gemacht.

Die Artikel von Roland Meighan und Alan Thomas rufen die überzeugenden Entschulungsargumente aus den 1970er Jahren wieder in Erinnerung, die damals gerade anfingen, die Ansichten über Bildung und Erziehung in England nachhaltig zu beeinflussen. Allerdings wurde diese Debatte in ihrer Fahrt von einem plötzlich erscheinenden schweren Gefährt, dem 'National Curriculum' (verpflichtende, landesweit einheitliche Lehrpläne) gebremst, das ausschließlich von institutioneller Bildung ausging. Meighan mahnt uns in zeitgemäßer Form, dass die Grundschule und die Sekundarschulen nur zwei Bausteine aus einer ganzen Palette von Möglichkeiten des Lehrens und des Lernens darstellen, welche für Kinder des 21. Jahrhunderts verfügbar sind. Thomas hingegen beleuchtet das beiläufige (informelle) Lernen, das ununterbrochen um uns herum stattfindet und sich in seinen Auswirkungen als weitaus erfolgreicher und nachhaltiger als herkömmlicher Schulunterricht erweist.

Traurig ist allerdings, dass es den Eltern in vielen Gegenden Europas immer noch nicht erlaubt ist, traditionellen Schulunterricht zurückzuweisen. Das gilt in besonderem Maße für Deutschland. Doch auch wo es gesetzlich geregelt und offiziell erlaubt ist, wie in Großbritannien und Frankreich, steht die Bildung ohne Schulbesuch ('home education', 'instruction en famille') nur allzu häufig unter Generalverdacht und wird zum Objekt rigoroser Kontrollen, die nach althergebrachten und größtenteils unangemessenen Schemata durchgeführt werden. Die Organisation, die ich vertrete, das 'Europäische Forum für Freiheit im Bildungswesen' ('European Forum for Freedom in Education') nimmt jegliche Versuche von Regierungen ernst, die darauf abzielen, das Recht der Eltern zu beschränken, über die Art des Bildungsweges ihrer Kinder zu entscheiden. Dieses Recht wird in den internationalen Vereinbarungen sowohl des Europarates als auch der Vereinten Nationen garantiert und wurde von nahezu allen europäischen Regierungen übernommen. Diejenigen, die Bildung ohne Schulbesuch verbieten, brechen nicht nur ihr eigenes Versprechen, die Wünsche der Eltern zu respektieren, sondern sie behindern fortan auch neue Wege in der Bildung und Erziehung von Kindern,welche für die ganze Gesellschaft positive Folgen haben könnten. Hoffentlich dauert es nicht mehr allzu lange, bis der Wahrheit der Durchbruch gelingt.

Introduction

by Leslie Safran Barson

Founding member of Learning Unlimited, a mother of two grown children who never went to school, organiser of a community centre for home educating families in central London, The Otherwise Club and currently finishing a PhD about home education and its significance for parents.

The idea for this book came from a perceived need of home educators across Europe to fight for the right of parents to educate their children in a way befitting the democratic principles espoused by European governments: that is, a way that gives learners prime control over their own education. To promote these ideas Learning Unlimited (LU) held a conference at Hes Fes, 2005 entitled Learner- Managed Learning in Europe. This book is the product of that conference.

The book falls into two sections; the first consists of an academic analysis of learner-managed learning from Dr. Meighan and Dr. Thomas, both academics working in the field of home education and learner-managed learning. The second reflects three European parents' experiences of home education and learner- managed learning from France, Germany and Switzerland, the difficulties they face in their respective countries, and how they manage to home educate using a learner-managed approach despite the legal and practical complications they face.

One of the problems we encountered in early meetings of LU was the different meanings of the word 'autonomous' as used in different European countries. In the UK the word 'autonomous' is used to cover an educational approach that is learner managed, with a concentration on conversational learning. It involves no set curriculum, time or space for learning but allows the learner to learn in a self-directed and self-assessed manner. Although the word 'autonomous' is Latin based and therefore used by many European cultures, a similarity in meaning and history of the word cannot be assumed. One way out of this problem was to try to find a replacement phrase that would not carry the ambiguity of the word 'autonomous' This is more difficult than it sounds as even in English this word stands for a whole set of principles rather than one clear meaning.

After much consideration the phrases 'informal learning' and 'learner-managed learning' were decided to be the best replacements. These phrases emphasise different aspects of this educational approach. 'Informal learning' stresses the non-directed and individualised nature of this approach as opposed to the more formal administered educational approach of school. The phrase 'learner-managed learning' emphasises the learners' control over their learning, whether that is informal or formal in nature. We chose that expression for the title of the book as it better conveys the educational ideas promoted here by all the speakers and portrays this approach as a positive educational theory. But in other parts of the book 'informal learning' better describes the experiences and so both terms are used throughout the book.

Another problem which has been encountered by the French and German speaking translators which was the adequate translation of the phrases "home-education", "home-educator" and "to home-educate". While there is one single English expression to cover a diversity of educational approaches and different life styles, a comparable phrase does not exist in either French or German. The translators had to find suitable phrases which in each case might have been different . Also, you will note that even within the German language there are differences in expression between the German language as spoken in Germany and as spoken in Switzerland.

In order to keep the lively spirit of the original speeches we have chosen to retain the style of speech and not try to force the speeches into lectures which have a dryer written form. Also for ease of style we chose not to put questions from the audience into the body of the text.

The home education information sections are for information purposes only. While we have made every effort to make sure the information is correct, we cannot be responsible for any mistakes. Anyone seeking legal advice is advised to get assistance from a solicitor who has some knowledge of home education in the country concerned.

We hope these articles inspire you to promote learner-managed learning and defend the rights of learners to be able to control their own learning, whatever their age.

Introduction

par Leslie Safran Barson

Membre fondateur de Learning Unlimited, Leslie Safran Barson est mère de deux enfants maintenant adultes qui n'ont jamais été scolarisés. Elle est organisatrice d'un centre de ressources et d'échange au centre de Londres : « The Otherwise Club » (le club autrement), pour des familles qui ont choisi d'instruire leurs enfants à la maison. Elle termine actuellement une thèse de doctorat dont le sujet de recherche porte sur l'instruction en famille et sa signification pour les parents.

L'idée de ce livre est née du besoin que ressentent des familles instruisant leurs enfants à la maison partout en Europe de défendre leur droit d'instruire leurs enfants conformément aux principes démocratiques adoptés par les gouvernements des pays européens : c'est-à-dire, en donnant d'abord à l'apprenant le contrôle de son instruction. Afin de promouvoir ces idées, *Learning Unlimited* (LU) a organisé une série de conférences à Hes Fes (Home Educators' Seaside Festival), 2005, ayant pour thème « L'apprentissage auto-géré en Europe ». Ce livre est le résultat de ces conférences.

Le livre comprend deux parties : la première comporte une analyse de l'apprentissage auto-géré, par le Dr Meighan et le Dr Thomas, tous deux universitaires ayant travaillé sur le thème de l'instruction à la maison et de l'apprentissage géré par l'apprenant, ou apprentissage auto-géré. La deuxième partie reflète l'expérience de trois parents européens dans ces domaines, en France, en Allemagne et en Suisse, les difficultés qu'ils rencontrent dans leurs pays respectifs et comment ils arrivent à gérer l'instruction à la maison en utilisant une approche d'apprentissage auto-géré, malgré les difficultés légales et pratiques qu'ils rencontrent.

Un des problèmes que nous avons rencontrés dans les premières réunions de LU était la signification du mot « autonome », tel qu'il est employé dans les différents pays européens. Au Royaume Uni, le mot « autonome » est employé pour décrire une approche éducative qui est gérée par l'apprenant et dont une composante importante est l'apprentissage par la discussion. Elle ne comprend ni un programme déterminé à l'avance, ni un moment ou un espace particulier pour apprendre, mais permet à l'apprenant de s'auto-diriger et de s'auto-évaluer. Bien que le mot « autonome » soit d'origine latine, et donc employé dans beaucoup de cultures européennes, on ne peut pas présumer une homogénéité de sa signification et de son histoire. Une solution était de trouver une phrase de remplacement pour éviter l'ambiguïté du mot « autonome ». Pas si facile, puisque même en anglais ce mot évoque tout un ensemble de principes plutôt qu'une seule signification claire.

Après beaucoup de réflexion, les expressions « apprentissage informel » et « apprentissage auto-géré » semblaient être les meilleurs substituts. Ces expressions soulignent différents aspects de cette même approche éducative : « l'apprentissage informel » met l'accent sur la nature non-dirigée et individualisée de cette approche, par opposition à l'approche plus formelle et autoritaire de l'école, tandis que l'expression « apprentissage auto-géré » souligne le contrôle que l'apprenant exerce sur son apprentissage, que sa nature soit informelle ou formelle. Nous avons choisi d'employer cette deuxième expression pour le titre du livre, parce qu'elle reflète mieux les idées sur l'éducation promues ici par tous les intervenants et donne l'image d'une théorie positive éducative. Mais dans certaines parties du livre « apprentissage informel » décrit mieux les expériences relatées et donc les deux expressions sont employées dans le livre.

Un autre problème rencontré par les traducteurs francophones et germanophones était la traduction adéquate des expressions « home education », « home educator » et « to home educate ». Alors qu'il existe une seule expression anglaise qui couvre une diversité d'approches et de modes de vie différents, une expression comparable n'existe pas en français ni en allemand. Les traducteurs ont donc été obligés de choisir des expressions appropriées qui peuvent varier de texte en texte. On peut aussi remarquer que même au sein de la langue allemande, il y a des expressions qui diffèrent entre la langue parlée en Allemagne et celle parlée en Suisse.

Afin de garder l'esprit vivant des interventions orales, nous avons choisi de préserver le style choisi par les intervenants plutôt que de les transformer en articles théoriques, ce qui donnerait une forme écrite plus aride. Nous avons également choisi pour faciliter la lecture de ne pas inclure dans le texte les questions posées par le public.

Les sections du livre donnant des informations générales sur l'instruction à domicile sont à but informatif uniquement. Bien que les informations données aient été vérifié le plus possible, nous ne pouvons être responsables quant aux erreurs éventuelles. Il est conseillé à toute personne cherchant une aide juridique de consulter un avocat ayant des connaissances sur l'instruction à domicile dans le pays concerné.

Nous espérons que ces articles vous inspireront l'envie de promouvoir l'apprentissage auto-géré et de défendre le droit des apprenants de diriger leur propre apprentissage, quelque soit leur âge.

Einführung

von Leslie Safran Barson

Gründungsmitglied von 'Learning Unlimited', Mutter zweier erwachsener Kinder, die nie zur Schule gingen, und Leiterin des kommunalen Zentrums 'The Otherwise Club' für Familien mit unbeschulten Kindern in Zentral-London. In Kürze wird sie ihre Doktorarbeit über Bildung zu Hause in Familieninitiative und deren Bedeutung für Eltern fertigstellen.

Familien, deren Kinder sich ohne Schulbesuch von zu Hause aus bilden, haben überall in Europa dasselbe Bedürfnis: Sie wollen für das Recht kämpfen, dass Eltern ihren Kindern Bildungswege ermöglichen können, die den demokratischen Grundsätzen angemessen sind, denen sich die europäischen Regierungen verpflichtet haben. Diese Erkenntnis brachte uns auf die Idee, das vorliegende Buch herauszugeben. Eine Bildung, die demokratischen Grundsätzen genügt, sollte so gestaltet sein, dass es in erster Linie die Lernenden selbst sind, die darüber entscheiden, wie sie sich bilden wollen. Um diesen Denkansatz zu fördern, veranstaltete 'Learning Unlimited' (LU) während des 'Hes Fes' ('Home Educators' Seaside Festival') des Jahres 2005 eine Konferenz zum Thema 'Selbstbestimmtes Lernen in Europa'. Diese Buch ist das Ergebnis dieser Konferenz.

Das Buch besteht aus zwei Teilen: Der erste Teil enthält wissenschaftliche Analysen von Dr. Meighan und Dr. Thomas zum Thema 'Selbstbestimmtes Lernen'. Beide Wissenschaftler arbeiten seit langem auf den Gebieten 'Bildung ohne Schulbesuch und in Familieninitiative' und 'Selbstbestimmtes Lernen'. Im zweiten Teil des Buches werden die Erfahrungen dreier Eltern – aus Frankreich, Deutschland und der Schweiz –

wiedergegeben, die ihren Kindern eine selbstbestimmte Bildung ohne Schulbesuch ermöglich(t)en. Sie berichten über die Schwierigkeiten, denen sie dabei in ihren Heimatländern ausgesetzt sind und darüber, wie es ihnen trotz rechtlicher und praktischer Hürden gelingt, ihre Kinder zu Hause frei und selbstbestimmt lernen zu lassen.

Eines der Probleme, mit dem wir schon bei den ersten Treffen von 'Learning Unlimited' konfrontiert wurden, besteht darin, dass das Wort 'autonom' in den verschiedenen europäischen Ländern unterschiedliche Bedeutungen hat. In Großbritannien steht der Ausdruck 'autonom' für einen Bildungsansatz, bei dem der Lernende sein Lernen selbst lenkt, wobei ein Schwerpunkt auf dem Lernen, das im Dialog mit anderen und mit dem Lebensumfeld des Lernenden geschieht, liegt. Dies bedeutet auch, dass es weder einen festen Lehrplan noch festgelegte Orte und Zeiten gibt, wodurch bestimmt würde, was, wie, wann und wo gelernt wird. Der Ausdruck 'autonom' impliziert, dass der Lernende selbst bestimmt und selbst bewertet, was und wie er lernt. Obwohl das Wort 'autonom' lateinischen Ursprungs ist und deshalb in vielen europäischen Sprachen benutzt wird, kann keine Übereinstimmung in der Bedeutung und Etymologie dieses Begriffs vorausgesetzt werden. Um diesem Dilemma zu entgehen, suchten wir nach einem passenden und eindeutigen Ausdruck, der den Begriff 'autonom' mit seiner Mehrdeutigkeit ersetzen könnte. Keine einfache Aufgabe, da der Begriff 'autonom' schon im Englischen eine ganze Bandbreite von Bedeutungen umfasst!

Wir haben uns eingehend damit beschäftigt herauszufinden, wie der Begriff 'autonom' am besten zu ersetzen wäre. Schließlich fiel die Entscheidung auf die Ausdrücke 'informal learning' (informelles, beiläufiges Lernen ohne Unterweisung) und 'learner-managed learning' (vom Lernenden selbst gesteuertes Lernen, selbstbestimmtes Lernen). Diese Ausdrücke heben verschiedene Facetten des freiheitlichen Bildungsansatzes, der Gegenstand unserer Betrachtung ist, hervor. 'Informelles Lernen' betont die ungelenkte, beiläufige und individuelle Natur des Lernens in lebendigen Zusammenhängen, im Gegensatz zum schulischen Lernen, das meist formal festgelegt und damit von 'oben' verwaltet ist. Der Ausdruck 'selbstbestimmtes Lernen' unterstreicht die Tatsache, dass der Lernende selbst die Kontrolle über sein Lernen behält, einerlei ob es eher spontaner, informeller oder festgelegter, formaler Natur ist. Für den Buchtitel wählten wir den Begriff 'selbstbestimmtes Lernen'. Er vermittelt präziser, welche

Vorstellungen von Bildung und Erziehung hier von den Vortragenden unterstützt werden. Zudem bringt der Begriff 'selbstbestimmtes Lernen' besonders treffend zum Ausdruck, dass der hier geschilderte freiheitliche Bildungsansatz geeignet ist, die bildungstheoretische Diskussion um einen positiven Aspekt zu erweitern. In anderen Teilen des Buches jedoch ist der Begriff 'informelles Lernen' besser geeignet, bestimmte Erfahrungen zu beschreiben. Deshalb werden in diesem Buch beide Begriffe nebeneinander benützt.

Ein weiteres sprachliches Problem trat bei der Übersetzung der englischen Texte ins Französische und ins Deutsche auf: Die englischen Begriffe 'home education', 'home educator' und 'to home educate' haben eine umfassende Bedeutung. Sie fassen in einem schlichten Ausdruck die verschiedensten Arten, wie Bildung ohne Schulbesuch gestaltet sein kann, zusammen – unabhängig von den dahinterstehenden pädagogischen Konzepten und den Formen ihrer praktischen Umsetzung. Im Französischen und im Deutschen hingegen existiert kein vergleichbares Wort. Die Übersetzer mussten passende, zum Teil wortreiche, umschreibende Ausdrücke finden. Da diese darüberhinaus dem jeweiligen Kontext angepasst sein müssen, wird man für die stets gleichen englischen Begriffe die unterschiedlichsten französischen und deutschen Wendungen finden. Selbst innerhalb des Deutschen gibt es kleine Unterschiede hinsichtlich der bundesrepublikanischen und der schweizerischen Wendungen.

Wir wollten gerne die Lebendigkeit der ursprünglichen Reden – wie sie auf dem 'Hes Fes' zu hören waren – in den Beiträgen dieses Buches erhalten. Wir haben uns daher entschieden die Beiträge weitgehend so zu veröffentlichen, wie sie – in freier Rede – gehalten wurden, anstatt sie in Form von Aufsätzen zu präsentieren, die in Schriftsprache verfasst und daher vermutlich trockener zu lesen gewesen wären. Ebenfalls aus stilistischen Gründen – um den Textfluss nicht zu unterbrechen – haben wir darauf verzichtet, die Fragen, die aus dem Publikum kamen, in direkter Rede in die Beiträge mit einzubeziehen.

Die Kapitel, in denen allgemeine Hinweise über Bildung zu Hause in den einzelnen Ländern gegeben werden, dienen ausschließlich der Information. Obwohl wir uns Mühe gegeben haben sicherzustellen, dass die gemachten Angaben richtig sind, können wir nicht für etwaige Fehler haften. Wenn Sie verlässliche rechtliche Auskünfte brauchen, sollten Sie die Hilfe eines

Anwalts bzw. einer Anwältin, die/der in Ihrem Land bereits einige Erfahrung in schulrechtlichen Fragen und insbesondere mit Bildung zu Hause hat, in Anspruch nehmen.

Wir hoffen, dass diese Beiträge Sie dazu anregen, das freie, selbstbestimmte Lernen zu unterstützen und die Rechte der Lernenden zu verteidigen, damit diese – ganz unabhängig von ihrem Alter – die Entscheidung dafür, was, wie, wann und wo sie lernen, selbst übernehmen können.

What Is and What Might Be:
Why many home-based educating families have found a learning system fit for a democracy

by Dr. Roland Meighan

Dr. Meighan now works as a writer and publisher. Previously he was Senior Lecturer in Education at the University of Birmingham and then Special Professor of Education at the University of Nottingham.

Learning Systems

When I began to look into learning systems, the first thing I found was that attempts to classify them were terrible! It needed work to make some sense of what they were made up of and what their logistics were. They include playgroups, nursery, infants, junior, secondary school, further education college, traditional universities, the Open University, the University of the Third Age, early childhood 'natural learning' at home, home-based education, Scouts, Guides, Woodcraft Folk, Duke of Edinburgh Award Scheme, the Public Library, learning clubs for Judo, Table Tennis, Tennis, Athletics, Dance, etc., Book Circles, learning co-operatives, community learning centres, the Army, Suicide Bombers Camps, and Terrorist Schools. Then there are schools, varying from the Danish EFTA residential model, to the City as School 'school without walls' approach, to the Summerhill democratic version, to that of the radical Sudbury Valley School, USA, to Canadian Cyber-schools, to Virtual Schools to Flexi-colleges. All these are learning systems and some of them can be very effective indeed.

For example, I was of a generation that had to do national service so I went to the army training camp and within about eight weeks they turned me into a potential killer! It is astonishing that this could happen. A mild mannered fellow like me, inclined to be a pacifist, at that time located within the Christian fold, can be turned into a killer in about eight weeks. But it is an astonishing learning system that turns ordinary folks into killers in a very short time by an intoxicating mix of personal threat and jingoism, *'are you a coward, then?'* and *'you should stand up for your country and be a patriot.'* A very clever psychological cocktail is built in there.

As a young teacher I was interested in learning systems because, having been not long out of school myself, I thought schooling was a pretty poor learning institution. I thought it might be a good idea to try to do something about it as a teacher. I used to tell people my real education did not take place at the Boys' Grammar school; it took place outside, in such places as the family, the neighborhood, the church, the youth club and the local library. They looked at me as though they thought I was mad, and my parents did not understand what I was on about, and, in the end, I gave up trying to explain and opted for mere endurance instead. But that meant when I went into teaching I tried to do something about it. I came across this table about the effectiveness of learning systems according to how much the learners actually remember.

	Average retention rate
Formal teaching	5%
Reading	10%
Audio-visual	20%
Demonstration	30%
Discussion Group	50%
Practice by doing	75%
Teaching others	90%
Immediate use of learning	90%

(Learning league table from National Training Laboratories, Bethel, Maine USA.)

It was an attempt to rank a number of learning systems according to how much the learners remembered afterwards. I found similar work from Canada, from Australia and later, from the Open University information learning technology unit

Right at the top of the list we see the average retention rate of formal learning is five percent! The immediate retention rate is greater. So if I gave you a test just after you read this you might retain ten percent, or even fifteen percent if we were lucky. But it drops to five percent over a week or two. That tells you something about what is wrong with our system. It relies on formal teaching enormously and yet it is only five percent efficient. Down in the middle of the list there is 'discussion group'. Another interpretation of that is 'purposive conversation'. Discussion group/purposive conversation is the main stay of home-based education. Is it any good? Well, it gets a fifty percent rating. So home-based educators should be confident in their approach and if they have any arguments with local education authorities (LEAs), show them these figures.

One problem was how to classify these learning systems and the classifications I came across were unhelpful. They said we have four types of learning systems. For example: teacher directed, teacher directed with more of a child centred approach; by which they mean child referenced; it is not child centred at all. Taking account of what you think the child wants is not child centred. Then there is sort of in-between half child referenced/child centred and half teacher directed. All four turned out to be classifications within one system, which is the first one I list below, the authoritarian view.

The **authoritarian** view can be summed up in the phrase *'you will do it our way or else'*. The 'or else' is critical because 'or else' is what drives the education policy of successive governments –'If you do not do it our way, we will find something nasty to do to you'. In the authoritarian education, in its various forms, one person or a small group of people, make and implement the decisions about what to learn, when to learn, how to learn, how to assess learning, and the learning environment. This is often all decided before the learners are recruited as individuals or meet as a group. As an exclusive method, it is favoured by totalitarian regimes because it aims to produce the conformist mentality. Teachers can easily learn to see themselves as 'miserable rule-followers', as one teacher put it.

A second view is the **autonomous,** (learner managed rather than uninvited teaching), approach to education, which can be summarized by the phrase, *'I did it my way'*. This can sound rather self indulgent, so I am suggesting it is actually more about *'I did it my way because I planned it and directed it but I did not ignore sources of advice or information or databases or the internet or public libraries, all there to help me make good decisions. In the end, however, I took charge of it. I did it my way.'*

3

A third view, the **democratic** view, is a variation on this theme: *'we did it our way.'* That is, we as a group decided to cooperate together, learn things together; we are autonomous people but we still think there is some mileage in the idea of cooperating and doing things as learning cooperatives.'

The fourth view is the **interactive way** *'we did it in a variety of ways'*. That sounds like a simple solution. You just pick bits and pieces from all the other three. But it is not that simple. The fundamental question is *'what is the default position'*? If there is any trouble or query or opposition, what does the education establishment default to?

In the past we have had people in the schooling system who have tried to push the authoritarian approach out of it into a bit of participation, a bit of democracy, a bit of autonomy, a bit of self-directed. They try to move an authoritarian system in an interactive direction. What happens when there start to be questions? What happens is that it defaults rapidly to *'you will do it our way or else'*! And we have experienced that in my lifetime. In 1988 the second national curriculum and the heavy testing and inspection regime pushed the learning system back a hundred years to replicate the ideas of the first national curriculum. It pushed it back solidly and brutally to *'you will do it our way or else'*.

So the interactive system is seductive in terms of being able to 'have a bit of each' system, but we must be vigilant. The important thing about an interactive system is where it starts. If you use the example of moving from the democratic system and incorporating autonomy and using some of the authoritarian forms, by invitation not by imposition, you can see how you are on safer ground than trying to move from the authoritarian system outwards. Any default will be back to the democratic system

Lessons from Looking at Learning Systems
A number of things come out of my study of learning systems. **First, there exists a variety of learning systems and each one produces different results.** It is worth reflecting on what kind of people, what

4

kind of mentality, is produced by 'you will do it our way or else'? Then, what kinds of people are produced by 'I did it my way'? Next, what kinds of people are produced by 'we did it our way in cooperation'? There are different mentalities that are absorbed from these systems.

What we want learning systems to do? I propose that the world's most pressing needs are for people who:
'Do not do any harm to each other,'
'Do no harm to the environment'
'Do no harm to themselves,'
and maybe even
'Do some good in the world if at all possible.'

In order to achieve those things, you need people who are autonomous, by that I mean people who are capable and confident researchers and democratically competent.

If those are our intentions, and I propose they should be, we have to design a learning system that gives us a chance of achieving them. The present system does no such thing. The mass coercive learning system called 'schooling' with endless uninvited teaching backed up with punishment and deterrents is not going to produce such people. It is going to produce people who, generally speaking, are used to the bullying mentality. Being themselves coerced, they are ready to coerce others if they get the chance. It may be bully with a small 'b' which is just to push people around, or it may be bully with a large 'B' which is being prepared to inflict your power on other people.

The second key lesson from looking at learning systems is that **how you learn is just as important as what you learn.** That is a lesson that has not been taken on board in the official thinking about education. Learning literacy in a bullying institution makes you a literate bully! If you want people who are literate and democratic, you are going to have to do it a different way! This was exemplified by the statement in a letter from a concentration camp survivor, who said "Reading, writing and arithmetic are important *only* if they serve to make our children more human" because in the

5

concentration camp he had seen some very highly qualified people involved in some very inhumane activities.

In fact, the 'final solution' was devised by the Nazis in a conference in which half the people who devised this genocide of supposed threatening groups in society, had PhDs. Having a PhD does not make you a decent human being; it might do something different. So we have to be careful about this. *How* you learn is as important, and may be more important, than *what* you learn.

Don Glines, of the Educational Futures Projects, USA, has made the rather provocative observation that the best traditional college graduates have perpetuated the majority of dilemmas facing society. It is the Oxford, Cambridge, Harvard and Yale graduates who are wrecking the environment – not all of them of course, but they are the people who run the unethical laboratories, they are the people who run the companies, they are the people who go for massive profits. (Glines, D. 1995, *Creating Educational Futures* Michigan: McNaughton and Gunn)

Even though yobs on the streets may be very irritating, the serious damage is not done by them. It is done by the people who have been through our institutions. If you want to point the finger of blame, you have to say, what are our systems like Oxford and Cambridge universities doing if they produce people who do these unprincipled things, these dangerous and lethal things? Our revered institutions may well be more part of the problem than they are part of the solution.

The third point that I learned from looking at learning systems is that **if you choose to operate a mass coercive standardized learning system; you are going, inevitably, to stifle and limit a lot of achievement** because you are trying to control people rather than educate them. Authoritarian systems are big on controlling people. Education comes very low down the agenda and that is not what the system is for. (As Winston Churchill observed, "*"Schools have not necessarily much to do with education ... they are mainly institutions of control where certain basic habits must be instilled in the young.*

Education is quite different and has little place in school." Sadly, he did not go on to say what we should do about it.)

When I first started to study home-based education in 1977, I was interested to see that the characteristics of home-based education were often quite different. and the outcomes were different. And indeed, some of the learning systems of home-based education were often much more like the systems that produce the genius. We have had various studies asking the question, 'how is the genius, the very high achieving people in society, actually produced?' The three factors below are from a study by Harold G McCurdy quoted in Leonard, G. B. (1970) *Education and Ecstasy*, London: John Murray:

1. "There is a high degree of attention given by parents and other adults, expressed in a variety of educational activities accompanied by abundant affection."
2. This one really worries people who run schools: "Only limited contact with other children outside the family, but plenty of contact with supportive adults." But we have set up an institution that has created peer groups where we can have maximum contact with people your own age, and here is a study saying 'if you want to produce high achievers, do not do that, do it differently!"
3. "An environment rich in, and supportive of, imagination and fantasy."

And McCurdy came to the shocking conclusion that the mass education system in the USA based on formal methods, coercion and inflexible education, constituted a vast experiment in reducing all these factors to the minimum. The result was the suppression of high achievement.

It is a mistake to think this is news. Edmond Holmes, Chief inspector of schools, writing in the early 1900s disowned the system of the first national curriculum and the aggressive inspection and testing service because he said he had come to the conclusion that he was ashamed of it and it was the tragedy of education to operate such a learning system.

7

Edmond Holmes made an interesting observation that the people running these systems may have good intentions. The leading actors in it, the parents and teachers who work along in this system, they are actually entailing the calamities of the human race without necessarily intending to. Not sensational calamities but the calamities that are deadly for their very unobtrusiveness. We accept them as our appointed lot. He listed these calamities thus: "perverted ideals, debased standards, contracted horizons, externalized aims, self-centred activities, weakened will power, lowered vitality, restricted and distorted growth and a profound misconception of the meaning of life." Even with the best of intentions, that is where this system ends up!

And the fourth lesson I learned from looking at learning systems is that **the next learning system will need to offer alternatives for everybody all the time,** just as home educators are tending to do already.

The Next Learning System: What is and What Might Be
This learning system does not yet exist, though there are elements to be seen in institutions like public libraries, museums, community arts schemes and the like. I have taken the title from Edmund Holmes' book *What Is and What Might Be* because he tried to define 'what might be'; in place of the system he felt was such a disaster. First of all we need to understand the system we have, so I tried to do that in this rather stark way.

If you look at an individual's journey in their younger years through the system, what does it look like? Well it looks like this; you start with a home-based education up to the age of five years. Then you attend a state school, with a government-dictated curriculum, testing and inspection, and a teacher-directed learning system, apart from small minorities who opt out or attend private schools (and they actually are only a variation of the same theme; it is still teacher-directed and it's still along the same kind of lines). That is what you get in the first year.

What do you get in the second year? The same. The next year? The same! The next year? The same! You just keep getting the *same* old recipe again and again and again. No wonder people talk about the dumbing-down effect of the learning system, if you are just going to be put through the same old procedures year after year until you get to 16. After that, some continue with the same, some leave school and go into employment. Some go on eventually into university and in university you get the same again! The university lecturers define the curriculum, they plan the courses and they teach it to you; your scope for actually developing yourself is pretty limited and only really starts if you do PhDs. Until then it is still an uninvited, imposed teaching regime.

That all sounds very gloomy, so it is important to add one or two riders of which this one from Everett Reimer in *School is Dead*, Harmondsworth: Pengiun, 1970, is very important for, as he says, *"some true educational experiences are bound to occur in schools and universities."* They occur, however, *despite* the system, not because of it. That is, there are teachers, there are lecturers, who try and swim against the tide of this oppressive system.

But there is something very temporary about their efforts. For example, I facilitated learning cooperatives in the university, along with Clive Harber, for 15 years. – the moment I left, they just faded away. People thought, *"Good, he's gone with that silly idea, we can just carry on telling them the stuff as before without distraction."* Indeed teacher training became even more restrictive because Ofsted [central government's Office for Standards in Education] made the kind of thing I was doing with Clive, of getting learners to plan in their learning cooperatives, more or less illegal. (See Harber, C. *Developing Democratic Education*, Ticknall: Education Now Books 1995) If lecturers now try that kind of thing they are told to stop it.

Arnold Wesker in his play *Roots* has one of his characters saying, as a kind of moment of enlightenment, *"but education is asking questions all the time."* It is an interesting view of education. But I suggest that the system does not encourage asking questions all the time. It encourages you to listen to the answers as defined by the system, to learn their answers and repeat them. The system does not encourage you to ask questions; it encourages you to ask the questions the system approves of. It is for this reason that people like

Paul Goodman have described the system I am talking about as *Compulsory Mis-education (* Penguin, 1971).

The first thing I think is to list what kind of episodes we could build into a learning programme. I do not mind what interval of time an episode takes – it can be a week, a month, or any time period. Here is a list of what you could build into it:

- Home education properly acknowledged and supported
- Home-based education learning cooperatives.
- Weekday programmes at community learning centres. These would be schools recycled into non-ageist centres that offer their programmes by invitation only. Not by compulsion, but by invitation.
- Weekend programs at local community learning centres. In other words, community led centres would open 8am - 8pm every day of the year.
- Travel and study year in the UK, or a travel and study year in Europe, or a travel and study year elsewhere.
- Use the residential colleges, again by invitation, to spend a year with an arts focus, or a music and dance focus, or a rural studies and environmental focus.
- A year exploring the locality of the learner and its learning sites. If you go in any kind of local tourist centre, there are racks of these learning possibilities in the locality, which you can go and visit and do things.
- Joining a democratic learning cooperative based on the local library. Libraries are probably one of the few learning institutions we could build on because they are invitational. They say, "here are some resources, we have organized them, you come and use them when you are ready." We could use the library as a basis for all sorts of groups including learning cooperatives.
- Join a city of schools scheme, and there is one these operating in Milton Keynes, where the youngsters decide they want to operate their learning at a certain age by having a series of mini-apprenticeships; using them as a base for learning about the world of employment and what

might be useful for them in terms of finding a career or finding a way of employment.

- A year on something like the Duke of Edinburgh's award scheme or the Scouts or the Guides or the Woodcraft. You could focus on that, not just on odd evenings, but for a sustained period of time.
- Voluntary work in the community
- Joining a virtual learning community programme, of which there are already several in existence such as notschool.net.

This list is not exhaustive. You could include other things like involvement in community arts projects. Community arts projects are a very important growth area at the moment in terms of the number of people who get involved in these and find they are giving them enormous satisfaction in learning things together.

I am sure you could add further options. These ideas are the building blocks, which could form the basis of one person's learning programme. But I do not need to work through these to build an individualised program. You could do your own version. What would you do if you could put the clock back? What would your learning program look like if you had this option to direct your own learning in episodes from the catalogue of possibilities?

The interesting thing is that this is, essentially, what home based educators do. What they do is not quite as formalized as this example but, actually, home educators tend to make up their own programme, searching around for elements to put in it, and some of the elements I have listed here do appear. But I would like to see that kind of approach available to everybody in the system. To do that, we are going to have to close schools as we know them. We are going to have to recycle the staff, the premises, and the resources into an invitational, community-based learning system.

My contact with many teachers suggests that they would *love* to be converted to such a system. Actually if only 8% of them are happy with the system they have got, according to a recent survey, by City and Guilds Survey reported in the *Guardian*, 25th Feb 2005, that means 92% of them are up for a better vision! *"Give us a vision that we could be proud of and involved in and our role will be a professional one instead of mechanics bolting on bits of knowledge onto people!"* In this system I am suggesting, the learners manage their learning progress by exercising choice, with support and guidance.

There is a lot of talk about choice and it is actually Hobson's choice when you look at it – you can choose from the few limited things we try to impose on you. Real choice would look much more open-ended. I am suggesting a personalized learning system. Using a system like this could move us into a new, exciting and vibrant educational landscape – one fit for a genuine democracy based on choices and opportunities!

I am sometimes asked how families who would like to home educate can do so without losing the benefits of the parents being in full time work. How can we change their minds, turn them round to our points of view?

The first thing I'd like to say in reply to that is that anything that's available in the system now can still be available, but it can be available by choice and not imposition. So if a family says "well look we've discussed this and for our purposes, for the time being this year at least, it would satisfy us if we could choose your programme 5 days a week from 9 o'clock to 4 o'clock and we've looked at the programme you're offering and we've found things which we could do and so we're actually happy if you could look after our children for those hours, that's how we can make our life work," and if that's what does the task for the family, then the family will choose it. But it's critical they choose it and it's not imposed from the centre. That is, if you want that kind of thing that works for you now, that's what you'll choose.

Will they then go on choosing the same thing again and again and again? There is a ray of hope here in a system in America called 'year round education'. A considerable number of schools in America are in the year round education movement and so as a development they offer a programme, every day of the year, 8 'til 8, right throughout the year except Christmas day. They then offer a series of packages to parents within that system. Packages in the summer, packages in the weekend, packages at the week time, summer packages, winter packages and so you can choose a package which will do something for you from this system. Now when they introduced this system in schools in America, the first thing is, the majority of parents, they stay with what they're familiar with. They say 'yeah thanks for offering us these things but we'd really like to do what we're familiar with: come on Monday, work through to Friday and then take a break. And we'd like to do term time, take a summer break, and come back again if that's all right with you." Fine that's what you've chosen, you know what's on offer. About 10% of the parents say 'no, actually, can we try some of these other things? We'd like to take our holiday break somewhere else, we'd like to take a break in the winter; we'd like to do the weekend courses and have a breather in the week day time.' And so there's a group of new pioneers who try out the new system. And what they found with this year round education offer in the parts of the States, it's not all over the States, is that the second year, the 10% is 20%, the third year, it's 40%, the fourth year, it's more than half the people now have started to take advantage of the choices. So I think there's the hopeful side – if you start giving people offers, they might be tentative at first but, when they see the other people have got something going, they think again, 'I want some of that.'

It's a contract, so there are set packages, but you can negotiate the contract. For example they say we run this course like this but if you want to do a modified version of it, we'll negotiate that. Families have chosen the contract. It isn't being chosen by central government saying, 'you will do this'. It is an offer, if you decide you don't want to do this thing, but you could do that thing, you contract to do it that's okay.

The role of exams in the next learning system of education is that they are on offer too. I think the model here is the Open University, which runs courses and says, you can do these courses but, by your own choice, you can just do the course for the fun of it with no assessment, you can do it and do some of the assessments for your own satisfaction but not be accredited, or you can do the assessment we've laid down and get the accreditation. In a sense, the Open

University has already been down this road where the learner decides how much assessment they want from this and if it's none 'that's okay, you just do it for the fun of it'.

Exams limit people's learning but it seems to me that they can limit people's learning for legitimate purposes. The crucial thing is that the learner should choose it, that is, you choose the package that includes the assessment and the accreditation. I'll give you an everyday example: I don't want somebody drilling my teeth, who hasn't been accredited. I want somebody to go to the course saying 'I wanted to be a dentist, I've done the course, I've passed the tests and you can have confidence in what I'm doing." So accreditation has a function. It's just that it goes wrong when it's imposed on a whole population: "You will *all* do the exam in Spanish!" "Why? For those who want to do the exam in Spanish, fine! But why impose it on everybody?

There is more information about community learning centres in a book produced in America called "Creating Learning Communities" (www.creatinglearningcommunities.org/resources/usa.htm), which goes into the examples we can find all around the globe. They're a bit tenuous but I think we have some examples of community learning centres and probably one of the best is home-educators who get together to organize learning cooperatives. Like the group on the Isle of Wight who organized the 'Learning Zone.' Forty families are operating a community learning centre there. They define it, they put their bid in for what they want to do, they see the catalogue they've produced, and they opt in and out of it. So we can already see the logistics of community learning centres in home education itself as well as in other things like community arts programs, which are doing this. But fundamentally a community learning centre looks basically like a school or a public library, but it is inviting people to use its facilities and not compelling them. Once you start introducing invitation into it, you begin to transform it.

Ce qui est et ce qui pourrait être: Pourquoi beaucoup de familles ayant choisi l'instruction à la maison ont trouvé un système d'apprentissage parfaitement adapté à la démocratie

par le Dr Roland Meighan

Le Docteur Meighan est à présent écrivain et éditeur. Il était auparavant maître-assistant en Sciences de l'Education à l'Université de Birmingham et ensuite professeur spécialisé en Sciences de l'Education à l'Université de Nottingham.

Systèmes d'apprentissage

Dès le début de mes recherches sur les systèmes d'apprentissage, j'ai constaté que les tentatives de classification de ces systèmes étaient mauvaises ! Il a fallu du travail pour donner un sens à la manière dont elles étaient constituées et à leur logique. Elles comprenaient les groupes de jeux, les crèches, les écoles maternelles, les écoles primaires, le collège, le lycée, les universités traditionnelles, « Open University », l'université du troisième âge, « l'apprentissage naturel » des bébés à la maison, l'instruction à la maison, les scouts, les guides, « Woodcraft Folk » (association pour la jeunesse), les bibliothèques, les clubs de judo, de tennis de table, de tennis, d'athlétisme, de danse, etc., les clubs de livres, les coopératives d'apprentissage, les centres d'enseignement collectifs, l'armée, les camps d'entraînement aux attentats suicides à la bombe et les écoles de terrorisme. Ensuite il y avait les écoles avec leurs différentes variations : le modèle résidentiel EFTA danois, le modèle où la ville est considérée comme « une école sans murs », la version démocratique de Summerhill, celle radicale de l'école de Sudbury Valley aux Etats-Unis d'Amérique, les cyber-écoles canadiennes, les écoles virtuelles, les flexi-universités. Tous ces modèles sont des systèmes éducatifs et certains peuvent être vraiment très efficaces.

Par exemple, je fais partie d'une génération qui a dû faire son service militaire et je suis donc parti à l'armée. En à peu près huit semaines, ils ont réussi à me transformer en un tueur potentiel ! Il est étonnant qu'une telle chose puisse se produire. Un garçon plutôt paisible comme moi, enclin au pacifisme et à cette époque partageant la foi chrétienne, peut être transformé en tueur en à peu près huit semaines. Mais c'est un système d'apprentissage étonnant qui transforme des gens ordinaires en tueurs en très peu de temps au moyen d'un mélange toxique de menace personnelle et de chauvinisme, « tu es donc un lâche ? » et « tu devrais défendre ton pays et être un patriote. ». Il se concocte un très savant cocktail psychologique là-dedans.

Jeune professeur, j'étais intéressé par les systèmes d'apprentissage parce que, fraîchement sorti de l'école, je pensais que c'était une institution plutôt médiocre. Je pensais que ce serait une bonne idée d'essayer de faire quelque chose à ce sujet en tant que professeur. J'avais l'habitude de dire aux gens que ma véritable formation n'avait pas eu lieu à l'école des garçons ; elle avait eu lieu dehors, au sein de la famille, du voisinage, de l'église, du club de jeunes, et à la bibliothèque de la ville. Ils me regardaient comme s'ils pensaient que j'étais fou, et mes parents ne comprenaient pas ce que je racontais. Finalement, j'ai tout simplement arrêté d'expliquer et j'ai décidé à la place d'opter pour une résistance passive. Mais dès que j'ai été nommé professeur, j'ai essayé de faire quelque chose. J'ai trouvé ce tableau sur l'efficacité des systèmes d'apprentissage mesurée par la quantité d'information réellement retenue par les étudiants.

	Taux moyen de mémorisation
Enseignement formel	5%
Lecture	10%
Audiovisuel	20%
Démonstration	30%
Groupe de discussion	50%
Pratique	75%
Enseigner à d'autres	90%
Utilisation immédiate de la connaissance	90%

(Tableau d'apprentissage des National Training Laboratories, Bethel, Maine USA.)

C'est un essai de classification de systèmes d'apprentissage selon la quantité d'information retenue par la suite. J'ai trouvé des études similaires au Canada, en Australie et, plus tard, au laboratoire de Sciences de l'Education de l'Université Ouverte (Open University).

Tout au début de la liste on peut voir que le taux moyen de mémorisation dans le cadre d'un enseignement formel est de cinq pour cent ! Le taux de mémorisation immédiate est plus élevé. Donc si je vous faisais passer un test juste après la lecture de ce texte, il se peut que vous en reteniez dix pour cent ou même quinze si l'on a de la chance. Mais ce taux baisse de cinq pour cent après une semaine ou deux. Cela montre bien ce qui ne va pas dans notre système. Il est en grande partie basé sur l'enseignement formel qui pourtant n'a un taux d'efficacité que de cinq pour cent. Au milieu de la liste, on peut lire « groupe de discussion », que l'on peut aussi appeler « conversation dirigée ». Les groupes de discussion / conversation dirigée sont les principaux éléments de l'instruction à la maison. Est-ce que c'est bien ? Eh bien, ils ont un taux de cinquante pour cent. Les parents qui instruisent à la maison devraient donc avoir confiance en leur approche et, s'ils ont des problèmes avec l'Education Nationale, leur montrer ces chiffres.

L'un des problèmes était de trouver un moyen pour classer ces systèmes d'apprentissage, et les classifications qui existaient déjà ne m'y aidèrent pas. Elles proposaient quatre types de systèmes d'apprentissage. Par exemple : le système dirigé par le professeur, celui dirigé par le professeur avec une approche plus centrée sur l'enfant ; ce par quoi ils voulaient dire en référence à l'enfant, ce qui ne veut pas dire centrée sur l'enfant : prendre en considération ce que vous pensez que l'enfant désire n'est pas être centré sur l'enfant. Il y a ensuite deux systèmes qui figurent entre les deux premiers : moitié en référence à l'enfant/centré sur l'enfant et moitié dirigé par le professeur. Tous les quatre sont finalement des classifications au sein d'un seul système qui est le premier que je présente ci-dessous, le système autoritaire.

Le système **autoritaire** peut se résumer par la phrase « *tu feras comme on te dit, sinon* ». Le « *sinon* » pose problème parce qu'il est ce qui conduit la politique de l'enseignement des gouvernements successifs – « *si tu ne fais pas ce qu'on te dit, on trouvera quelque chose de déplaisant à te faire* ». Dans l'éducation autoritaire sous toutes ses formes, une personne ou un petit groupe de personnes prennent et mettent en œuvre les décisions concernant le choix des connaissances, le moment de l'apprentissage, la façon dont on apprend, dont on mesure l'apprentissage, et l'environnement d'apprentissage. Tout est souvent complètement décidé avant même que les étudiants ne soient recrutés individuellement ou avant qu'ils ne se rencontrent. Les régimes totalitaires favorisent cette méthode unique parce qu'elle vise à produire des mentalités conformistes. Les professeurs peuvent facilement apprendre à se voir eux-mêmes comme de « pauvres suiveurs de règles », comme l'a dit un professeur.

Le deuxième système est l'approche **autonome** de l'apprentissage (celui-ci est dirigé par l'apprenant au lieu d'être un enseignement imposé), qui peut se résumer par la phrase « *je l'ai fait à ma façon* ». Ce qui peut paraître assez auto-complaisant, je propose donc plutôt « *je l'ai fait à ma façon parce que je l'ai organisé et géré, mais j'ai tenu compte des sources de conseils ou d'information, des bases de données, d'Internet, des bibliothèques, tous là pour m'aider à prendre les bonnes décisions. Finalement, cependant, j'en ai pris la responsabilité, je l'ai fait à ma façon.* ».

Le troisième système, le **démocratique**, est une variation sur le thème : « *on l'a fait à notre façon* ». C'est-à-dire que nous, en groupe, avons décidé de coopérer, d'apprendre ensemble ; nous sommes autonomes mais nous valorisons la coopération et le regroupement en coopératives d'apprentissage.

Le quatrième système est le système **interactif** « *on l'a fait de diverses façons* ». Cette solution a l'air simple. Il suffit de ramasser ici et là des morceaux des trois autres systèmes. En fait ce n'est pas si simple. La question fondamentale est « *quelle est la position de repli ?* » S'il y a des problèmes, des doutes ou des oppositions, que fait l'Education Nationale ?

Dans le passé, certains enseignants ont essayé de transformer l'approche autoritaire en y ajoutant un peu plus de participation, un peu de démocratie, un peu d'autonomie, un peu d'autogestion. Ils ont essayé de donner au système autoritaire une direction interactive. Que se passe-t-il quand les problèmes arrivent ? Ce qui se passe est que ça se transforme vite en « *tu le fais comme on te dit, sinon !* » Et nous l'avons vécu à mon époque. En 1988, le second programme national ainsi que les nombreux contrôles et le régime d'inspections ont fait reculer le système d'apprentissage d'une centaine d'années pour reproduire les idées du premier programme national. Il l'a fortement et brutalement renvoyé á « *tu vas le faire comme on te dit, sinon* ».

Le système interactif nous séduit donc par sa capacité à prendre 'un peu de chaque' système, mais nous devons être vigilants. La chose la plus importante pour un système interactif est de savoir où il commence. Si vous prenez l'exemple dans lequel on quitte le système démocratique pour incorporer l'autonomie et utiliser un peu d'autorité, en invitant et non pas en imposant, vous pouvez constater que vous êtes sur un terrain plus confortable que si vous essayez de partir du système autoritaire. Tout repli vous ramènera vers le système démocratique.

Leçons tirées de l'étude des systèmes d'apprentissage
Mon étude des systèmes d'apprentissage fait apparaître plusieurs choses. **Premièrement, il existe une grande variété de systèmes d'apprentissage et chacun produit des résultats différents.** Cela vaut la peine de réfléchir sur quel genre de personnes, quel genre de mentalités sont produits par le « tu le feras comme on te dit, sinon » ? Ensuite, regardons quels genres de personnes sont produits par le « je l'ai fait à ma façon » ? Puis, quels genres de personnes sont produits par « nous l'avons fait à notre façon en coopération » ? Des mentalités différentes découlent de chaque système.

Qu'attendons-nous des systèmes d'enseignement ? J'ai dans l'idée que ce dont le monde a le besoin le plus urgent, c'est de personnes qui :
- ne font aucun mal aux autres,
- ne font pas de tort à l'environnement,
- ne se font pas de mal,
et même peut-être :

- font du bien dans le monde si cela est possible.

Pour parvenir à cela, on a besoin de personnes autonomes, et je veux dire par là des personnes qui soient des chercheurs capables et confiants, et qui aient une bonne compétence démocratique.

Si ce sont nos intentions, et je propose qu'elles le soient, nous devons créer un système d'éducation qui nous donne une chance d'y parvenir. Le système actuel n'y parvient pas. Le système d'enseignement de contrainte des masses appelé 'école', avec une succession sans fin d'enseignements imposés, appuyés par des punitions et d'autres moyens dissuasifs, ne va pas produire de telles personnes. Il va produire des gens qui, de manière générale, sont habitués à la mentalité tyrannique. Etant eux-mêmes contraints, ils sont prêts à contraindre les autres s'ils en ont l'opportunité. Il se peut que ce soit juste de la tyrannie avec un petit t, qui consiste juste à mener la vie dure aux autres, ou il se peut que ce soit de la tyrannie avec un grand T, qui consiste à être prêt à imposer son pouvoir sur d'autres personnes.

La seconde leçon clef tirée de l'étude des systèmes d'enseignement est que **la façon dont vous apprenez est aussi importante que ce que vous apprenez.** C'est une leçon qui n'a pas été examinée avec attention dans les réflexions officielles concernant l'éducation. Apprendre à lire et à écrire dans une institution tyrannique fait de vous un tyran instruit ! Si vous voulez des personnes qui soient instruites et démocrates, vous allez devoir faire différemment ! Un exemple en est donné par le survivant d'un camp de concentration qui écrivit : « La lecture, l'écriture et l'arithmétique sont importants *uniquement* s'ils servent à rendre nos enfants plus humains », parce que dans le camp de concentration, il avait vu des gens hautement qualifiés impliqués dans des activités très inhumaines.

En fait, les nazis ont créé « la solution finale » au cours d'un congrès dont la moitié des participants, qui travaillaient donc à bâtir ce génocide de groupes supposés menaçants pour la société, avaient un doctorat. Avoir un doctorat ne vous transforme pas en être humain respectable ; cela peut même faire quelque chose de complètement différent. Nous devons donc être prudents à ce propos. *La façon* dont vous apprenez est aussi importante, voire peut-être plus importante, que *ce que* vous apprenez.

Don Glines, de Educational Futures Projects, USA, a fait cette observation plutôt provocatrice : les élèves sortis des meilleurs grandes écoles traditionnelles ont contribué à perpétuer la majorité des problèmes de notre société. Ce sont les étudiants sortis d'Oxford, de Cambridge, de Harvard et de Yale qui détruisent l'environnement – pas tous bien sûr, mais ils sont les dirigeants des laboratoires sans éthique, ils sont les dirigeants des entreprises, ils sont les personnes qui recherchent de gros profits. (Glines, D. 1995, *Creating Educational Futures* Michigan; McNaughton and Gunn).

Même si les petits caïds de la rue nous irritent, ce ne sont pas eux qui font les gros dégâts. Ce sont les gens qui sortent de nos institutions. Si vous voulez savoir sur qui rejeter la faute, vous devez vous demander : que font des systèmes comme les universités d'Oxford et de Cambridge quand ils produisent les auteurs de ces actes dénués de principe, ces actes dangereux et mortels ? Il se peut que nos institutions vénérées soient plus partie prenante du problème que de la solution.

La troisième leçon tirée de mon étude des systèmes d'apprentissage est que **si vous choisissez de faire marcher un système éducatif de masse standardisé et coercitif, vous allez, inévitablement, empêcher et limiter en grande partie les réussites possibles**, parce que vous essayez de contrôler les gens plutôt que de les éduquer. Les systèmes autoritaires excellent à contrôler les personnes. L'instruction arrive bien plus bas sur leur liste et ce n'est pas le but du système. (Comme Winston Churchill l'avait observé : « *les écoles n'ont pas forcément grand-chose à voir avec l'instruction... ce sont principalement des institutions de contrôle au sein desquelles certaines habitudes de base doivent être implantées dans nos jeunes enfants. L'instruction est très différente et a peu de place dans l'école* ». Malheureusement, il n'a pas continué et expliqué ce que nous devrions faire à ce propos.).

Quand, en 1977, j'ai commencé à étudier l'instruction à la maison, j'ai été surpris de constater que les caractéristiques, ainsi que les résultats, étaient souvent très différents de ceux de l'instruction traditionnelle. En fait, certains des systèmes d'apprentissage utilisés dans l'enseignement à la maison étaient souvent beaucoup plus semblables aux systèmes qui produisent des génies. Il existe différentes études pour tenter de répondre à la question : « comment produit-on les génies, les personnes qui réussissent exceptionnellement bien dans notre société ? ». Les trois facteurs ci-dessous proviennent d'une étude menée par Harold G. McCurdy citée dans Leonard, G.B. (1970) *Education and Ecstasy*, (Education et extase), London, John Murray :

1. « Beaucoup d'attention est donnée par les parents et d'autres adultes, et s'exprime dans une grande variété d'activités éducatrices, accompagnées de beaucoup d'affection. ».

2. Le point suivant inquiète beaucoup les personnes qui dirigent les écoles : « Un contact limité avec des enfants en dehors de la famille, mais beaucoup de contacts avec des adultes qui apportent leur soutien. » Alors que nous avons mis en place une institution qui a créé des groupements par âge, dans lesquels nous avons un maximum de contact avec les gens du même âge, voici une étude qui dit : « si vous voulez produire des gens qui réussissent, ne faites pas cela, faites autrement ! ».

3. « Un environnement qui apporte à profusion et qui encourage imagination et fantaisie. ».

Et McCurdy en est arrivé à la conclusion surprenante que le système d'enseignement de masse aux Etats Unis, basé sur des méthodes formelles, la coercition et un enseignement rigide, constituait une vaste expérience dans laquelle ces facteurs sont réduits au minimum. Le résultat en est l'absence de grandes réussites.

Ce serait une erreur de penser que tout ceci est nouveau. Edmond Holmes, inspecteur principal des écoles, écrivait au début des années 1900 qu'il désavouait le système du premier programme national, et l'agressivité des inspections et des examens, parce qu'il en était arrivé à en avoir honte. Il pensait que c'était une tragédie pour l'enseignement qu'il soit réalisé selon ces méthodes.

Edmond Holmes avait fait l'intéressante remarque qu'il était possible que les personnes qui dirigent ces systèmes aient de bonnes intentions. Les principaux acteurs de ce système, les parents et les professeurs qui y travaillent ensemble, sont en réalité en train de générer les désastres de la race humaine, sans en avoir nécessairement l'intention. Ce ne sont pas des désastres phénoménaux mais ils sont dangereux par leur discrétion même. Nous les acceptons comme notre lot quotidien. Edmond Holmes a fait la liste de ces désastres : « idéaux pervertis, niveaux abaissés, horizons rétrécis, objectifs imposés de l'extérieur, activités centrées sur soi-même, volonté affaiblie, baisse de vitalité, croissance restreinte et déformée, et conception profondément fausse du sens de la vie ». Même avec les meilleures intentions, c'est à cela que ce système aboutit !

La quatrième leçon qui ressort de l'étude des systèmes d'enseignement est que **le prochain système éducatif devra offrir des alternatives pour tout le monde à tout moment,** exactement ce vers quoi les éducateurs à la maison tendent déjà.

Le prochain système éducatif: Ce qui est et ce qui pourrait être
Ce système éducatif n'existe pas encore, bien que l'on en devine les prémisses dans les institutions telles que les bibliothèques, les musées, les centres d'activités artistiques et autres du même genre. J'ai utilisé un titre tiré du livre d'Edmund Holmes, *What Is and What Might Be* (ce qui est et ce qui pourrait être) parce qu'il a essayé de définir 'ce qui pourrait être' à la place du système qu'il qualifie de désastreux. Tout d'abord nous devons comprendre notre système actuel, j'ai donc essayé de m'y employer de manière assez radicale.

Si l'on regarde le parcours dans ce système d'un être humain dans ses jeunes années, à quoi cela ressemble-t-il ? Eh bien cela ressemble à ceci : on commence avec des apprentissages à la maison jusqu'à l'âge de cinq ans. Ensuite on va dans une école publique, avec un programme dicté par le gouvernement, des inspections et des examens, et un système d'enseignement dirigé par le professeur. Mise à part une faible minorité qui choisit de ne pas aller á l'école ou qui va dans des écoles privées (qui sont en fait une variation sur le même thème ; c'est toujours dirigé par le professeur et c'est toujours dans le même style), c'est ce qui se passe la première année.

Que se passe-t-il la seconde année ? La même chose. L'année suivante ? pareil ! L'année suivante ? pareil ! On continue avec la *même* vieille recette encore et encore. Il n'est pas étonnant que l'on parle de l'effet abrutissant du système éducatif, si l'on nous fait passer par les même vieilles procédures année après année jusqu'à seize ans. Après cela, certains continuent sur le même chemin, d'autres quittent l'école et entrent sur le marché du travail. Certains continuent jusqu'à l'université et c'est encore la même chose ! Les maîtres-assistants définissent le programme, ils préparent les cours et les enseignent ; les possibilités de développement personnel sont assez limitées et ne commencent réellement qu'au niveau du doctorat. Avant le doctorat, c'est toujours un régime d'enseignement non demandé et imposé.

Ce tableau semble plutôt sombre, il est donc important d'ajouter une ou deux petites notes. La première, d'Everett Reimer dans *School Is Dead* (L'école est morte), Harmondsworth ; Pengiun, 1970, est très importante parce que, comme il l'écrit, *« des expériences réellement éducatives ont forcément lieu dans les écoles et les universités »*. Elles ont lieu, cependant, *en dépit* du système, et non pas grâce à lui. C'est-à-dire qu'il y a des enseignants, des maîtres-assistants, qui essayent de nager à contre-courant de ce système oppressif.

Il y a cependant quelque chose d'extrêmement provisoire dans leurs efforts. Par exemple, j'ai aidé à développer, avec Clive Harver, des coopératives d'apprentissage au sein de l'université, et ceci pendant 15 ans. – Dés que je suis parti, elles ont disparu. Les gens ont pensé, *« Bien, il est parti, lui et son idée saugrenue, nous pouvons donc continuer à leur dire les choses comme avant, sans être dérangés. »*. De fait, la formation des professeurs devint même encore plus restrictive parce que l'Ofsted (bureau central du gouvernement pour les normes dans l'éducation) rendit le genre de chose que je faisais avec Clive - permettre aux étudiants de planifier leur apprentissage dans leurs coopératives - plus ou moins illégal. (Voir Harber, C. *Developing Democratic Education,* (Développer une éducation démocratique), Ticknall: Education Now Books 1995). Si des

24

maîtres-assistants essayent aujourd'hui ce genre de chose, on leur demande d'arrêter.

Arnold Wesker dans sa pièce de théâtre 'Roots' (Racines) fait dire à l'un des ses personnages, qui vient d'avoir une révélation : *« mais l'apprentissage, c'est poser des questions tout le temps ! ».* C'est une vision de l'apprentissage intéressante. Je pense cependant que le système n'encourage pas à poser des questions tout le temps. Il vous encourage à écouter les réponses définies par le système, à apprendre ces réponses et à les répéter. Le système ne vous encourage pas à poser des questions ; il vous encourage à poser les questions qu'il approuve. C'est la raison pour laquelle des gens comme Paul Goodman nomment le système dont je parle *Compulsory Miseducation* (Mauvaise éducation obligatoire) (Penguin 1971).

La première chose, je pense, est de faire la liste des différentes phases qui pourraient faire partie d'un programme d'apprentissage. La durée des phases m'importe peu – ce peut être une semaine, un mois ou quelque durée que ce soit. Voici la liste de ce que vous pourriez y trouver :

- Education à la maison dûment reconnue et soutenue.
- Coopératives d'enseignement à la maison.
- Programmes pendant la semaine dans des centres d'enseignement collectifs. Ceux-ci seraient des écoles recyclées en centres, sans discrimination d'âge, qui inviteraient juste à suivre leurs programmes. Non pas en obligeant, mais en invitant à venir.
- Programmes de week-end dans les centres d'enseignement collectifs. Autrement dit, les centres dirigés par la collectivité seraient ouverts de 8 heures du matin à 8 heures du soir tous les jours de l'année.
- Une année de voyage d'étude au Royaume-Uni. Ou une année de voyage d'étude en Europe. Ou une année de voyage d'étude ailleurs.
- Utilisation des grandes écoles et universités, à nouveau sur un mode d'invitation, pour faire une année de spécialisation

en art ou en danse ou en musique, ou en études rurales et de l'environnement.

- Une année pour explorer la région d'origine de l'apprenant et ses lieux d'apprentissage. Dans toutes les maisons du tourisme on trouve des rangées de prospectus sur les possibilités et lieux d'apprentissage locaux, que l'on peut visiter et où l'on peut faire des choses.
- Se joindre à une coopérative d'apprentissage démocratique basée sur la bibliothèque locale. Les bibliothèques sont probablement l'une des rares institutions d'apprentissage sur lesquelles nous pourrions compter puisqu'elles fonctionnent sur un mode non obligatoire. Elles disent : « voici quelques ressources, nous les avons organisées, vous venez les utiliser quand vous êtes prêts. ». Nous pourrions utiliser les bibliothèques comme base pour toutes sortes de groupes, y compris les coopératives d'apprentissage.
- Rejoindre un 'projet de ville d'écoles', il y en a un qui est en fonction à Milton Keynes, dans lequel les jeunes décident à un moment donné qu'ils veulent faire leur formation par une série de mini-apprentissages. Ils les utilisent comme base pour apprendre le monde du travail et ce qui pourrait leur être utile dans la recherche de leur métier ou dans la recherche d'emploi.
- Une année sur un projet comme le prix du Duc d'Edinburgh, ou les Scouts, ou les Guides, ou « Woodcraft » (association britannique pour la jeunesse). Il serait possible de s'y consacrer, non pas juste quelques soirées de temps en temps, mais de manière intensive sur une certaine durée.
- Travail collectif volontaire.
- Se joindre à un programme collectif d'enseignement virtuel, dont certains existent déjà, comme par exemple notschool.net.

Cette liste n'est pas exhaustive. On pourrait ajouter d'autres choses comme la participation à des projets artistiques de groupe. Ces activités artistiques sont actuellement en pleine croissance. De plus en plus de personnes s'y engagent et trouvent énormément de satisfaction à apprendre des choses ensemble.

Je suis sûr que l'on pourrait ajouter d'autres options. Ces idées sont des blocs de construction qui pourraient former la base du programme d'enseignement d'une personne. Je n'ai cependant pas besoin de les utiliser pour créer un programme individualisé. Vous pourriez faire votre propre version. Que feriez-vous si vous pouviez remonter le temps ? A quoi ressemblerait votre cursus de formation si vous aviez la possibilité de diriger votre propre apprentissage en séquences puisées dans le catalogue des possibilités ?

Il est intéressant de remarquer que c'est essentiellement ce que font les parents qui enseignent à la maison. Ce qu'ils font n'est pas aussi formalisé que dans cet exemple, mais ils ont quand même tendance à créer leur propre programme, en cherchant des éléments autour d'eux, et certains éléments de ma liste en font effectivement partie. Mais j'aimerais que cette approche soit disponible pour tous ceux qui sont dans le système. Pour arriver à cela, nous allons devoir fermer les écoles telles que nous les connaissons. Nous allons devoir transformer le personnel, les locaux et les ressources en un système éducatif non obligatoire basé sur la collectivité.

Mes contacts avec de nombreux professeurs suggèrent qu'ils seraient *ravis* d'être convertis à un tel système. En fait, si seulement 8% d'entre eux sont contents du système actuel, selon une étude récente réalisée par City and Guilds Survey et mentionnée dans le *Guardian* du 25 Février 2005, cela veut dire que 92% d'entre eux sont prêts pour une meilleure vision des choses ! *« Donnez-nous une vision dont nous pourrions être fiers, et dans laquelle nous pourrions nous impliquer en professionnels, au lieu d'être des mécaniciens qui assemblent des bouts de savoir dans la tête des élèves! »*. Dans le système que je propose, les apprenants gèrent leur progression en faisant des choix, avec du soutien et des conseils.

On parle beaucoup de choix mais si l'on regarde de plus près, c'est en fait un choix de Hobson, un faux choix : vous pouvez choisir parmi le peu de choses que l'on essaye de vous imposer. Un choix véritable serait beaucoup plus flexible. Je propose un système d'enseignement personnalisé. L'utilisation d'un tel système pourrait nous transporter dans un nouveau paysage éducatif, excitant et plein de vie - un système parfait pour une véritable démocratie basée sur des choix et des opportunités !

Certains parents, dont les enfants aimeraient être instruits à la maison, ne choisissent pas cette option parce qu'ils veulent garder les bénéfices du travail à plein temps, l'argent. Comment pouvons-nous les aider à changer d'avis, les convaincre de notre point de vue ?

La première chose que j'aimerais dire en réponse à cela est que tout ce qui est disponible aujourd'hui dans le système le serait toujours, mais par choix et non en étant imposé. Donc, si une famille dit : « eh bien, nous avons discuté de cela et dans notre cas, pour cette année en tout cas, nous serions heureux de bénéficier de votre programme 5 jours par semaine de 9 heures à 16 heures. Nous avons regardé le programme que vous offrez et nous avons trouvé des choses qui nous conviennent, nous serions donc heureux si vous pouviez vous occuper de nos enfants pendant ces heures-là, c'est ce qui nous conviendrait le mieux », et si cela correspond aux besoins de la famille, alors la famille le choisira. Mais il est essentiel qu'ils le choisissent et non pas qu'il leur soit imposé. C'est-à-dire que si ce que vous voulez c'est ce qui marche bien pour vous maintenant, alors c'est ce que vous choisirez.

Continueront-ils à choisir les mêmes choses encore et encore ? Il y a une lueur d'espoir à ce sujet dans le système américain appelé 'l'école toute l'année'. Un nombre considérable d'écoles américaines fait partie du mouvement 'l'école toute l'année', et proposent donc un programme tous les jours de l'année, de 8 heures du matin à 8 heures du soir, tout au long de l'année, sauf le jour de Noël. Elles offrent aussi tout un choix de cursus au sein de ce système : formations pendant l'été, le week-end, la semaine, l'hiver... Vous pouvez donc choisir, dans ce système, le cursus qui vous convient. Lorsque ce système fut introduit dans les écoles aux Etats-Unis, la première réaction de la majorité des parents fut de garder ce à quoi ils étaient habitués. Ils disaient : « Ah! Merci de nous proposer tout cela, mais nous aimerions faire ce que nous avons l'habitude de faire : venir le lundi, travailler jusqu'au vendredi et nous reposer ensuite. Et nous aimerions que ce soit sous forme de trimestres, des vacances en été, et revenir ensuite, si vous êtes d'accord ». Parfait, c'est ce que vous avez choisi, vous savez ce qui est disponible. Environ 10% des parents disaient : « voyons, en fait, pourrions-nous essayer certaines autres choses ? Nous aimerions prendre nos vacances à un autre moment, nous aimerions prendre un congé en hiver, nous aimerions prendre des cours le week-end et souffler un peu pendant la semaine ». Et donc un groupe de pionniers se forme et essaye le nouveau système. Et ce qui apparaît dans les endroits qui proposent cette 'école toute l'année' (il n'y en a pas dans tous les Etats-Unis), c'est que la deuxième année les 10% deviennent 20%, 40% la troisième année, et la quatrième année, plus de la moitié des parents commencent à utiliser les possibilités de choix. Je pense donc qu'il y a de l'espoir – si vous commencez à donner le choix aux familles, il se peut qu'elles hésitent au début, mais en voyant que les autres autour d'elles se sont lancées, elles penseront finalement : « je veux essayer aussi. ».

C'est un contrat, il y a donc des cursus tout préparés, mais vous pouvez négocier le contrat. Par exemple, le cours est prévu d'une telle façon, mais si vous voulez en faire une version modifiée, nous pouvons le négocier. Ce sont les familles qui choisissent le contrat. Ce n'est pas le gouvernement central qui l'a choisi en disant : « vous ferez ceci. ». C'est une offre, si vous décidez que vous ne voulez pas faire ceci, mais plutôt cela, vous passez un contrat pour le faire, il n'y a pas de problème.

Dans le prochain système d'éducation, les examens seront aussi en option. Je pense que dans ce domaine, le modèle est l'Université Ouverte, qui propose des cours et dit : « vous pouvez suivre ces cours, mais vous pouvez faire le choix de les suivre juste pour votre plaisir et sans examen, ou vous pouvez les suivre et passer quelques examens pour votre satisfaction personnelle, mais sans obtention de diplôme, ou vous pouvez passer les examens que nous organisons et obtenir les diplômes. ». D'une certaine manière, l'Université Ouverte est déjà dans une voie qui permet à l'étudiant de choisir le niveau d'évaluation qu'il souhaite, et s'il n'en veut aucune : « pas de problème, tu le fais juste pour le plaisir. ».

Les examens limitent l'apprentissage, mais il me semble que ce peut être pour des raisons légitimes. Le plus important est que l'étudiant puisse choisir, c'est-à-dire choisir le cursus qui comprend l'examen et le diplôme. Voici un exemple dans la vie de tous les jours : je ne veux pas que quelqu'un sans diplôme me triture les dents. Je veux que ce soit quelqu'un qui a suivi les cours en disant : « je voulais être dentiste, j'ai suivi la formation, j'ai passé les examens et vous pouvez avoir confiance dans ce que je fais. ». L'examen a donc une fonction. Il perd juste son sens quand il est imposé à toute une population : « Vous allez *tous* passer cet examen d'espagnol ! ». « Pourquoi ? Ceux qui souhaitent passer l'examen d'espagnol, très bien ! Mais pourquoi l'imposer à tout le monde ? ».

On peut trouver plus d'information sur les « centres d'enseignement collectifs » dans un livre américain dont le titre est « Creating Learning Communities » (Créer des centres d'enseignement collectif   www.creatinglearningcommunities.org/resources/usa.htm) qui fait le tour des exemples qu'on peut trouver de par le monde. Même s'ils ne sont pas nombreux, je pense que nous avons quelques exemples de centres d'enseignement collectifs, et l'un des meilleurs est probablement celui de groupes de parents qui instruisent à la maison et qui se rassemblent pour organiser des coopératives d'enseignement. Comme le groupe qui a organisé une 'zone d'enseignement sur l'île de Wight'. Quarante familles y dirigent un centre d'enseignement collectif. Elles le définissent, elles inscrivent leurs souhaits, elles étudient le catalogue qu'elles ont produit, et elles y puisent ce qui les intéresse. Nous pouvons donc déjà voir la logistique des centres d'enseignement collectifs au travers de l'instruction à la maison, et aussi dans d'autres structures, comme les centres d'activités artistiques qui font la même chose. Fondamentalement, un centre d'enseignement collectif ressemble à une école ou une bibliothèque, mais il invite les personnes à utiliser ses équipements, il ne les y oblige pas. A partir du moment où vous y introduisez l'idée que ce n'est pas obligatoire, vous commencez à le transformer.

Was Ist und Was Sein Könnte:
Warum viele Familien, bei denen Bildung von zuhause aus stattfindet, ein einer Demokratie angemessenes Bildungssystem gefunden haben

von Dr. Roland Meighan

Dr. Meighan arbeitet jetzt als Autor und Verleger. Vorher war er Dozent für Erziehungswissenschaft (Senior Lecturer in Education) an der Universität Birmingham und dann Professor für Erziehungswissenschaft (Special Professor of Education) an der Universität Nottingham.

Bildungssysteme

Als ich begann, Nachforschungen über Bildungssysteme anzustellen, fand ich als erstes heraus, dass die Versuche, sie zu klassifizieren, furchtbar waren! Es erforderte einigen Aufwand, ihren Aufbau und ihren inneren Zusammenhang zu verstehen. Zu ihnen gehören Spielgruppen, Kinderkrippen, Kindergärten, Grundschulen, weiterführende Schulen, Einrichtungen der Erwachsenenbildung, traditionelle Universitäten, die Fernuniversität, die Seniorenuniversität, natürliches Lernen zuhause in der frühen Kindheit, Bildung ohne Schulbesuch von zuhause aus („home-based education"), Pfadfindergruppen, „Woodcraft Folk" (Jugendorganisation in Großbritannien) , „Duke of Edinburgh Award Scheme" (ein Programm zur Förderung der Persönlichkeitsentwicklung von Jugendlichen durch gesellschaftliche und sportliche Aktivitäten), öffentliche Bibliotheken, Vereine für Judo, Tischtennis, Tennis, Tanz, Sportvereine, Literaturkreise, Lerngemeinschaften, gemeinschaftliche Lernzentren, die Armee, Ausbildungslager für Selbstmordattentäter und Terroristen-Schulen. Dann gibt es Schulen, die vom dänischen EFTA-Internat über den Ansatz der ‚Stadt als Schule' („Schulen ohne Wände"), die demokratische Variante Summerhill, die radikale Sudbury Valley School in den USA, kanadische Internet-Fernschulen und virtuelle Schulen bis zu „Flexi-colleges" reichen. All das sind Bildungssysteme und einige von ihnen können tatsächlich sehr wirksam sein.

Ich, zum Beispiel, entstamme einer Generation, die Wehrpflicht zu leisten hatte, also ging ich in ein Armee-Trainingslager und innerhalb von acht Wochen machten sie aus mir einen potentiellen Mörder. Es ist erstaunlich, dass dies passieren konnte. Ein sanftmütiger, zum Pazifismus neigender Kerl wie ich, damals Mitglied einer christlichen Kirchengemeinde, kann innerhalb von acht Wochen in einen Mörder verwandelt werden. Es ist wirklich ein erstaunliches Bildungssystem, das gewöhnliche Leute in kurzer Zeit durch eine berauschende Mischung aus persönlicher Bedrohung, Hurrapatriotismus, *„du bist wohl ein Feigling!"* und *„du musst Patriot sein und für dein Land stehen!"* in Mörder verwandelt. Es besteht aus einem ausgeklügelten psychologischen Cocktail.

Als junger Lehrer war ich an Bildungssystemen sehr interessiert, denn ich, der ich selbst noch nicht lange aus der Schule war, hielt Schulen für eine ziemlich armselige Bildungseinrichtung. Ich hielt es für eine gute Idee, als Lehrer zu versuchen, etwas dagegen zu tun. Ich erzählte den Leuten, dass meine wirkliche Bildung nicht im Knabengymnasium stattfand; sie fand außerhalb statt, wie zum Beispiel in der Familie, der Nachbarschaft, der Kirche, dem Jugendclub und der Stadtbibliothek. Sie schauten mich an, als ob ich verrückt sei und meine Eltern verstanden nicht, worum es mir ging. Letztendlich gab ich die Versuche auf es zu erklären und bat stattdessen lediglich um Geduld. Es führte aber dazu, dass ich mich aufmachte etwas daran zu ändern, als ich mit meiner Lehrertätigkeit anfing. Ich entdeckte diese Tabelle zur Effektivität von Bildungsmethoden, gemessen an dem, was der Lerner tatsächlich erinnert.

	Durchschnittlich erinnerter Anteil
formaler Unterricht	5%
Lesen	10%
Hören und Sehen (audio-visuell)	20%
Vorführung (Demonstration)	30%
Diskussion in der Gruppe	50%
praktische Tätigkeit	75%

Belehrung Anderer	90%
sofortige Anwendung des Gelernten	90%

(Learning league table from National Training Laboratories, Bethel, Maine, USA)

Dies war ein Versuch, eine Anzahl von Bildungsmethoden anhand dessen zu ordnen, wie viel die Lerner anschließend erinnern. Ich fand ähnliche Untersuchungen aus Kanada und aus Australien und später von der „Open University information learning technology unit".

Ganz oben auf der Liste sehen wir, dass der durchschnittlich erinnerte Anteil nach formalem Unterricht fünf Prozent beträgt! Der kurzfristig erinnerte Anteil ist höher. Wenn ich Ihnen, direkt nachdem Sie dies gelesen haben, hierzu Fragen stellen würde, würden Sie sich an etwa zehn Prozent oder mit etwas Glück sogar an fünfzehn Prozent erinnern. Aber innerhalb von ein bis zwei Wochen geht der erinnerte Anteil bis auf fünf Prozent zurück. Dies verrät Ihnen etwas darüber, was an unserem System falsch ist. Es beruht zum größten Teil auf formalem Unterricht und daher beträgt die Effizienz nur 5%. Weiter unten in der Mitte der Liste findet sich die „Diskussion in der Gruppe". Eine andere Bezeichnung hierfür ist „zielgerichtetes Gespräch". Die Diskussion in der Gruppe bzw. das zielgerichtete Gespräch ist die Hauptgrundlage der Bildung von zuhause aus. Ist dies sinnvoll? Nun ja, damit wird ein Wert von fünfzig Prozent erreicht. Familien, in denen Bildung ohne Schulbesuch stattfindet, sollten also ihrem Ansatz vertrauen, und wenn es Auseinandersetzungen mit den örtlichen Schulbehörden gibt, dann zeigt ihnen diese Zahlen.

Ein Problem war die Frage, wie diese Bildungssysteme klassifiziert werden können, und die Klassifizierungen, auf die ich stieß, waren nicht hilfreich. Es wurden vier Typen von Bildungssystemen unterschieden. Beispielsweise: lehrergeführt, lehrergeführt mit einem mehr kindzentrierten Ansatz; dabei ist kindbezogen gemeint, es ist in keiner Weise kindzentriert. Zu berücksichtigen, was man denkt, was das Kind will, ist nicht kindzentriert. Dann gibt es noch den Zwischentyp, halb kindbezogen/kindzentriert und halb lehrergeführt. Alle vier erschienen als Klassifizierungen innerhalb eines Systems, unten als erstes aufgeführt, nämlich das der autoritären Auffassung.

Die **autoritäre** Auffassung kann mit der folgenden Formulierung beschrieben werden: „*Du wirst es auf unsere Art tun, sonst ...*". Das „sonst ..." ist entscheidend, denn dieses „sonst ..." bildet die Grundlage der Bildungspolitik erfolgreicher Regierungen – „Wenn du es nicht auf unsere Art tust, dann werden wir etwas Übles finden, das wir dir antun können." In der autoritären Bildung mit ihren unterschiedlichen Ausprägungen trifft eine Person oder eine kleine Gruppe von Personen die Entscheidungen darüber, was gelernt wird, wann gelernt wird, wie gelernt wird, wie Lernen beurteilt wird und über die Lernumgebung und diese Person oder Gruppe setzt diese Entscheidungen durch. Dies alles wird oft entschieden, bevor die einzelnen Lerner ausgewählt werden oder sich als Gruppe treffen. Als ausschließliche Methode wird sie von totalitären Regimes bevorzugt, weil sie angepasstes Verhalten fördert. Lehrer können leicht in die Situation geraten, sich selbst als ‚erbärmliche Befolger von Vorschriften' zu sehen, wie ein Lehrer es ausdrückte.

Eine zweite Auffassung ist der **selbstständige** Bildungsansatz (eher eigene Planung des Lerners als ungebetene Belehrung). Er kann durch die Formulierung „*Ich habe es auf meine Art gemacht.*" zusammengefasst werden. So könnte es als sehr eigennützig und maßlos verstanden werden, daher schlage ich eher folgende Beschreibung vor: „*Ich habe es auf meine Art gemacht, weil ich es selbst geplant und gesteuert habe, aber ich habe dabei keine Quelle von Ratschlägen oder Informationen oder das Internet oder öffentliche Bibliotheken übergangen, all dies hilft dabei, gute Entscheidungen zu treffen. Letztendlich habe ich all das berücksichtigt. Ich habe es auf meine Art gemacht.*"

Eine dritte, die **demokratische** Auffassung ist eine Abwandlung dieses Motivs: „*Wir haben es auf unsere Art gemacht.*" Das heißt, wir als Gruppe haben beschlossen zusammenzuarbeiten, Dinge gemeinsam zu lernen; wir sind eigenständige Menschen, aber dennoch glauben wir, dass es nützlich ist, zusammenzuarbeiten und so etwas wie Lerngemeinschaften einzurichten.

Die vierte Auffassung ist der **interaktive** Ansatz: „*Wir haben es auf eine Vielzahl verschiedener Arten gemacht.*" Das klingt nach einer einfachen Lösung. Man nimmt einfach ein paar Splitter und Bruchstücke der drei anderen. Aber es ist nicht so einfach. Die Grundfrage ist: „*Was ist die Vorgabe?*" Wenn es irgendwelche Schwierigkeiten oder Beschwerden oder Widerspruch gibt, was gibt die Bildungseinrichtung dann vor?

Es gab Menschen im Schulsystem, die versuchten, den autoritären Ansatz aus ihm zurückzudrängen zugunsten von ein bisschen Mitwirkung, ein bisschen Demokratie, ein bisschen Autonomie, ein bisschen Selbstbestimmung. Sie versuchen, ein autoritäres System in Richtung eines interaktiven Ansatzes zu bewegen. Was passiert, wenn dort Fragen auftauchen? Was tatsächlich passiert, ist, dass die Vorgabe sehr schnell umkippt in „*Du wirst es auf unsere Art tun, sonst ...*". Wir haben das bereits mehrfach erlebt. 1998 warfen die zweiten landesweit einheitlichen Bildungspläne und das umfangreiche Überprüfungs- und Inspektionsprogramm das Bildungssystem um hundert Jahre zurück zu dem Gedankengut der ersten landesweit einheitlichen Bildungspläne. Sie warfen es massiv und brutal zurück zu „*Du wirst es auf unsere Art tun, sonst ...*".

Der interaktive Ansatz ist also verlockend durch seine Möglichkeit, „von jedem System ein bisschen was" zu haben, aber wir müssen wachsam sein. Die entscheidende Sache bei einem interaktiven System ist der Startpunkt. Wenn man beispielsweise die Entwicklung eines demokratischen Systems betrachtet, in das Selbstständigkeit und die Anwendung einiger autoritärer Verfahren aufgrund einer Bitte aufgenommen werden, nicht von Zwang, dann kann man sehen, dass man sich auf sichererem Boden bewegt, als bei dem Versuch, aus einem autoritären System heraus eine Veränderung zu bewirken. Im ersten Fall wird jede Vorgabe zurück zum demokratischen System führen.

Schlussfolgerungen aus der Betrachtung von Bildungssystemen
Aus meinen Studien über Bildungssysteme ergibt sich eine Reihe von Feststellungen. **Erstens gibt es eine Reihe verschiedener Bildungssysteme und jedes davon führt zu anderen Ergebnissen. Es** lohnt sich, darüber nachzudenken, welche Art Menschen, welche Grundeinstellungen durch „Du wirst es auf unsere Art tun, sonst ..." hervorgebracht werden. Und welche Art Menschen wird durch „Ich

habe es auf meine Art gemacht." hervorgebracht? Weiter, welche Art Menschen wird durch „Wir haben es gemeinsam, durch Zusammenarbeit, auf unsere Art gemacht." Es sind unterschiedliche Grundeinstellungen, die aus diesen Systemen erwachsen.

Was erwarten wir von Bildungssystemen? Ich behaupte, was die Welt am dringendsten braucht, sind Menschen, die:
‚sich nicht gegenseitig verletzen',
‚die Umwelt nicht schädigen',
‚sich selbst nicht verletzen'
und vielleicht sogar
‚in der Welt etwas Gutes vollbringen, falls überhaupt möglich'.

Um dies zu erreichen, brauchen wir selbstständige Menschen, darunter verstehe ich Menschen, die fähige und souveräne Forscher sind und demokratische Kompetenz besitzen.

Wenn dies unsere Ziele sind, und ich meine dass sie es sein sollten, dann müssen wir ein Bildungssystem entwickeln, das uns eine Möglichkeit bietet, sie zu erreichen. Das derzeitige System tut dies nicht. Das „Schule" genannte System der verpflichtenden Massenbildung mit unendlicher unerbetener Belehrung, unterstützt durch Bestrafungen und Abschreckungsmittel, wird keine solchen Menschen hervorbringen. Es wird Menschen hervorbringen, die, allgemein gesprochen, an einen tyrannischen Umgang gewöhnt sind. Sie stehen selbst unter Zwang, daher sind sie bereit, andere zu zwingen, wenn sich die Gelegenheit bietet. Es kann „kleingeschriebene Tyrannei" sein, was einfach bedeutet, andere herumzuschubsen, oder es kann „großgeschriebene Tyrannei" sein, was die Bereitschaft zur Ausübung von Macht über andere Menschen bedeutet.

Die zweite entscheidende Erkenntnis aus meinen Studien über Bildungssysteme ist, dass **WIE man lernt genauso wichtig ist, wie WAS man lernt**. Diese Erkenntnis wird in der amtlichen Auffassung von Bildung nicht berücksichtigt. Der Erwerb von Bildung innerhalb einer tyrannischen Institution macht den Menschen zu einem gebildeten Tyrannen! Wenn man gebildete und demokratische Menschen haben möchte, muss man einen anderen Weg wählen. Dies wird durch die Feststellung eines Überlebenden eines Konzentrationslagers verdeutlicht, der sagte: „Lesen, schreiben und rechnen sind *nur* dann wichtig, wenn sie helfen, unsere Kinder menschlicher werden zu lassen." In dem Konzentrationslager hatte er einige sehr hoch qualifizierte Menschen erlebt, die an sehr unmenschlichen Handlungen beteiligt waren.

Tatsache ist, dass die „Endlösung" von den Nationalsozialisten in einer Konferenz beschlossen wurde, wobei die Hälfte der Personen, die diesen Völkermord an vermeintlich bedrohlichen Gruppen der Gesellschaft beschlossen, einen Doktortitel besaß. Im Besitz eines Doktortitels zu sein, macht einen nicht zu einem anständigen Menschen, es kann auch anderes bewirken. Wir müssen daher in diesem Punkt vorsichtig sein. *WIE* man lernt ist genauso wichtig, und vielleicht noch wichtiger, als *WAS* man lernt.

Don Glines von *„Educational Futures Projects"* („Projekte zur Zukunft der Bildung"), USA, hat die ziemlich provokante Beobachtung gemacht, dass die besten Absolventen der traditionellen Hochschulen den größten Teil der Probleme fortführen, mit denen die Gesellschaft konfrontiert ist. Es sind Absolventen von Oxford, Cambridge, Harvard und Yale, die die Umwelt zerstören – natürlich nicht alle von ihnen, aber sie sind diejenigen, die die skrupellosen Labore betreiben, sie sind diejenigen, die die Firmen leiten, sie sind diejenigen, die die gewaltigen Gewinne anstreben. (Glines, D. 1995, *Creating Educational Futures* Michigan: NcNaughton and Gunn)

Rowdys auf den Straßen mögen beängstigend sein, aber die schwerwiegenden Schäden werden nicht von ihnen verursacht. Sie werden von Menschen verursacht, die unsere Bildungseinrichtungen durchlaufen haben. Wenn man einen Schuldigen sucht, muss man die Frage stellen, was unsere Hochschulen tun, wenn sie Menschen mit einem so gewissenlosen, gefährlichen und tödlichen Verhalten hervorbringen? Unsere hoch geachteten Bildungseinrichtungen könnten durchaus eher ein Teil des Problems denn ein Teil der Lösung sein.

Die dritte Erkenntnis aus meinen Studien über Bildungssysteme ist: **Wenn man sich dazu entscheidet, ein System einer verpflichtenden Massenbildung zu betreiben, wird man unvermeidlich einen großen Teil der möglichen Leistung begrenzen, ja ersticken, weil** man eher versucht, die Menschen zu kontrollieren, als sie zu bilden. Autoritäre Systeme sind groß darin, Menschen zu kontrollieren. Bildung erscheint erst sehr weit unten auf dem Programm und sie ist nicht der Zweck des Systems. (wie Winston Churchill bemerkte: *"Schulen haben nicht notwendigerweise viel mit Bildung zu tun ... sie sind hauptsächlich Kontrolleinrichtungen, in denen den jungen Menschen bestimmte grundlegende Verhaltensweisen eingetrichtert werden. Bildung ist etwas gänzlich anderes und hat in Schulen kaum Platz."* Leider führte er nicht weiter aus, was dagegen zu tun wäre.)

Als ich 1977 begann, mich mit Bildung ohne Schulbesuch zu beschäftigen, nahm ich mit großem Interesse wahr, dass die Merkmale der Bildung ohne Schulbesuch oft deutlich anders waren, und auch die Ergebnisse davon waren anders. Tatsächlich waren einige der dabei angewandten Bildungsmethoden den Methoden sehr ähnlich, die hohe Begabungen hervorbringen. In verschiedenen Studien war die Frage aufgeworfen worden, wie hohe Begabungen, wie gesellschaftlich besonders erfolgreiche Menschen hervorgebracht werden. Die drei unten aufgeführten Faktoren stammen aus einer Studie von Harold G. McCurdy und werden in Leonard, G. B. (1970) *Education and Ecstasy*, London: John Murray zitiert:

1. „Es gibt ein hohes Maß an Aufmerksamkeit von Eltern und anderen Erwachsenen, das sich in einer Vielzahl von Bildungsaktivitäten, verbunden mit starker Zuneigung ausdrückt."
2. Dieser Faktor bringt Betreiber von Schulen wirklich in Schwierigkeiten: „Nur begrenzter Kontakt mit anderen Kindern außerhalb der Familie, aber viel Kontakt mit unterstützenden Erwachsenen." Wir aber haben eine Einrichtung geschaffen, in der Jahrgangsgruppen entstehen, in denen man den größtmöglichen Kontakt mit Menschen gleichen Alters hat, und es gibt eine Studie, die besagt: ‚Wenn Sie höchst leistungsfähige Menschen haben wollen, tun sie das nicht, machen Sie es auf andere Weise.'
3. „Eine Umgebung, die Vorstellungskraft und Phantasie bietet und fördert."

McCurdy kam zu dem erschreckenden Schluss, dass das System der Massenbildung in den USA, beruhend auf formalen Unterrichtsmethoden, Zwang und unflexibler Erziehung, den gewaltigen Versuch darstellte, alle diese Faktoren auf ein Minimum zu reduzieren. Das Ergebnis war die Unterdrückung von hohen Leistungen.

Es ist ein Irrtum, dies für eine neue Erkenntnis zu halten. Der leitende Schulinspektor Edmond Holmes lehnte in seinen um 1900 erschienenen Schriften das System der ersten landesweit einheitlichen Bildungspläne ab, weil er sagte, er sei zu dem Ergebnis gekommen, sich hierfür schämen zu müssen und der Betrieb eines solchen Bildungssystems stelle eine Tragödie für die Bildung dar.

Edmond Holmes machte die Beobachtung, dass die Menschen, die diese Bildungssysteme betreiben, durchaus gute Absichten haben mögen. Ihre Hauptakteure, die Eltern und die in diesem System arbeitenden Lehrer, verursachen Unheil für die Menschheit, ohne es zu beabsichtigen. Kein Aufsehen erregendes Unheil, aber ein Unheil, welches aufgrund seiner Unaufdringlichkeit tödlich ist. Wir akzeptieren es als das uns bestimmte Schicksal. Er führte als Aspekte dieses Unheils auf: pervertierte Werte, verminderte Anforderungen, eingeschränkte Sichtweisen, auf Äußerliches gerichtete Ziele, egozentrisches Verhalten, geschwächte Willenskraft, verminderte Lebensfreude, begrenztes und verzerrtes Wachstum, sowie ein grundlegendes Missverständnis über den Sinn des Lebens." Sogar mit den besten Absichten wird das System dahin führen!

Die vierte Erkenntnis aus meinen Studien über Bildungssysteme ist, **dass das nächste Bildungssystem allen Menschen jederzeit Alternativen anbieten muss**, genau das wozu Familien, in denen Bildung von zuhause aus stattfindet, heute schon neigen.

Das nächste Bildungssystem: Was Ist und Was Sein Könnte

Dieses Bildungssystem existiert noch nicht, obwohl Elemente davon bereits in Einrichtungen wie öffentlichen Bibliotheken, Museen, kommunalen Kunst-Programmen und ähnlichem zu finden sind. Ich habe den Titel aus Edmond Holmes Buch „Was Ist und Was Sein Könnte" (*What Is and What Might Be*) übernommen, weil er versuchte, zu bestimmen, was „sein könnte"; an Stelle des Systems, welches er als eine Katastrophe empfand. Zuerst müssen wir das System, das wir haben, verstehen, also versuchte ich es auf diese möglichst sachliche Weise.

Wenn man den Weg einer Einzelperson in jungen Jahren durch das System betrachtet, wie stellt er sich dar? Nun, er sieht folgendermaßen aus: Man beginnt mit Bildung von zuhause aus bis zum Alter von fünf Jahren. Dann besucht man eine öffentliche Schule mit einem durch die Regierung diktierten Lehrplan, Überprüfungen und Kontrollen und einer lehrerzentrierten Lernmethode, abgesehen von kleinen Minderheiten, die aussteigen oder private Schulen besuchen (und diese sind in Wirklichkeit nur eine Abwandlung desselben Themas; sie sind ebenso lehrerzentriert und folgen denselben Grundprinzipien). So sieht das erste Schuljahr aus.

Wie sieht das zweite Schuljahr aus? Genauso. Das nächste Jahr? Genauso! Es bleibt dabei, dass *dasselbe* alte Rezept wieder und wieder und wieder angewandt wird. Es erstaunt nicht, dass vom verdummenden Effekt des Bildungssystems gesprochen wird, wenn man sich jedes Jahr, bis man 16 ist, denselben alten Prozeduren unterziehen muss. Danach machen einige genauso weiter, andere verlassen die Schule und gehen in ein Arbeitsverhältnis. Manche gehen auf die Universität und dort geht es genauso weiter! Die Dozenten der Universität legen die Studienpläne fest, sie planen die Kurse und sie unterrichten; der Spielraum für eine eigene Entwicklung ist sehr begrenzt und existiert genau genommen erst während der Promotion. Bis dahin handelt es sich um ein von außen aufgeprägtes, beherrschendes System des unerbetenen Unterrichts.

Das alles hört sich sehr bedrückend an und daher ist es wichtig, einige Ergänzungen hinzuzufügen, von denen diejenige von Everett Reimer in „*School is dead*", Penguin, 1970, besonders wichtig ist, denn er sagt: „*einige echte Bildungserfahrungen können nur in Schulen und Universitäten stattfinden.*" Sie treten aber *trotz* des Systems auf, nicht seinetwegen. Das heißt, es gibt Lehrer und Dozenten, die es wagen, gegen den Strom dieses unterdrückenden Systems zu schwimmen.

Aber ihre Bemühungen sind sehr kurzlebig. Beispielsweise unterstützte ich gemeinsam mit Clive Harber 15 Jahre lang Lerngemeinschaften in der Universität – sobald ich gegangen war, verschwanden sie einfach. Die Leute dachten: „*Fein! Er ist mit seiner verrückten Idee verschwunden, jetzt können wir ungestört weiter unseren Stoff unterrichten.*" Tatsächlich wurde die Lehrerausbildung wesentlich stärker reglementiert, denn durch OFSTED (Office for Standards in Education – zentrales Regierungsamt für Bildungsstandards in Großbritannien) wurde das, was ich mit Clive getan hatte, nämlich Lernende dazu zu bringen in Lerngemeinschaften zu planen, mehr oder weniger illegal gemacht. (Siehe Harber, C. *Developing Democratic education*, Ticknall: Education Now Books, 1995) Wenn Dozenten jetzt so etwas versuchen, fordert man sie auf, es zu unterlassen.

In seinem Theaterstück „*Roots*" („Wurzeln") lässt Arnold Wesker eine seiner Personen wie in einem Augenblick der Erleuchtung sagen: „*aber Bildung bedeutet, ständig Fragen zu stellen.*" Dies ist eine sehr interessante Auffassung von Bildung. Ich behaupte aber, dass unser Bildungssystem nicht dazu ermutigt, ständig Fragen zu stellen. Man wird dazu gebracht, auf die vom System festgelegten Antworten zu hören, diese Antworten zu lernen und wiederzugeben. Es ermutigt nicht dazu, eigene Fragen zu stellen; es ermutigt dazu, die Fragen zu stellen, die das System gutheißt. Aus diesem Grund wurde das System über das ich spreche, von Menschen wie Paul Goodman als „verpflichtende Fehl-Bildung" (*Compulsory Miseducation*; Penguin, 1971) bezeichnet.

Der erste Schritt ist meiner Ansicht nach aufzulisten, welche Bausteine ein Bildungsprogramm ergeben könnten. Die zeitliche Dauer eines solchen Bausteins ist für mich unerheblich – es könnte eine Woche, ein Monat oder ein jeglicher anderer Zeitabschnitt sein. Hier ist eine Liste von möglichen Punkten:

- Regelrecht anerkannte und unterstützte Bildung von zuhause aus.
- Lerngemeinschaften von Menschen, die sich ohne Schulbesuch bilden.

- Angebote an Wochentagen in gemeinschaftlichen Lernzentren. Dies könnten Schulgebäude sein, welche in Einrichtungen ohne Altersbeschränkung umgewandelt werden und nur Angebote auf freiwilliger Basis bieten. Nicht verpflichtend, sondern als Angebote.
- Wochenend-Angebote in gemeinschaftlichen Lernzentren. Mit anderen Worten, die von Städten und Gemeinden betriebenen Zentren wären das ganze Jahr über täglich von 8 Uhr morgens bis 8 Uhr abends geöffnet.
- Ein Reise- und Studienjahr in Großbritannien, oder ein Reise- und Studienjahr in Europa oder ein Reise- und Studienjahr sonstwo auf der Welt.
- Nutzung der örtlichen Hochschulen, wiederum als freiwilliges Angebot, um sich ein Jahr lang mit einem der Schwerpunkte Kunst, Musik und Tanz oder Umweltschutz zu beschäftigen.
- Ein Jahr zur Erkundung des Wohnorts des Lerners und der dortigen Bildungseinrichtungen. Wenn man in irgendeine Art Fremdenverkehrsbüro geht, findet man dort Regale voller Bildungsmöglichkeiten in der Umgebung, die man besuchen und nutzen kann.
- Mitgliedschaft in einer der örtlichen Bibliothek angegliederten Lerngemeinschaft. Bibliotheken sind möglicherweise eine der wenigen Bildungseinrichtungen, auf die man aufbauen könnte, denn es sind freiwillige Angebote. Dort heißt es: „Hier gibt es eine Reihe von Materialien, wir haben sie bereitgestellt und geordnet, jeder kann kommen und sie benutzen, wenn er dazu bereit ist." Wir könnten die Bibliotheken als Basis für verschiedenste Gruppen, einschließlich Lerngemeinschaften, benutzen.
- Teilnahme an einem „Stadt der Schulen"-Modell (city of schools scheme), so etwas gibt es in Milton Keynes, wo sich Jugendliche in einem bestimmten Alter entschließen, ihre Bildung in Form einer Reihe von „Schnupper-Ausbildungen" zu gestalten, sie benutzen diese als Grundlage, um mehr über das Arbeitsleben zu erfahren und herauszufinden, was ihnen in Bezug auf die Berufswahl und die Arbeitsplatzsuche nützlich sein könnte.
- Ein Jahr mit etwas Ähnlichem wie dem „Duke of Edinburgh Award Scheme" oder bei den Pfadfindern oder dem „Woodcraft

Folk". Man könnte so etwas als Schwerpunkt wählen, nicht nur für einige Abende, sondern für einen längeren Zeitraum.

- Freiwillige Arbeit für die Gemeinde
- Teilnahme an einem „virtuellen", internetbasierten Lerngemeinschaftsprogramm, wovon bereits einige existieren, wie www.notschool.net

Diese Liste ist nicht erschöpfend. Man könnte weitere Bausteine wie die Teilnahme an kommunalen Kunstprojekten einfügen. Kommunale Kunstprojekte sind ein sehr wichtiger Wachstumsbereich im Hinblick auf die Zahl der Personen, die sich beteiligen und in dem gemeinsamen Lernen eine enorme Befriedigung finden.

Ich bin sicher, dass sich noch viel mehr Möglichkeiten finden lassen. Diese Ideen sind Bausteine, die die Grundlage eines persönlichen Bildungsprogramms sein können. Aber ich muss nicht alle durchgehen, um ein eigenes Bildungsprogramm zu gestalten. Jeder kann seine eigene Version leben. Was würden Sie tun, wenn Sie die Zeit zurückdrehen könnten? Wie würde Ihr Bildungsprogramm aussehen, wenn Sie die Möglichkeit hätten, Ihre eigene Bildung mit Bausteinen aus diesem Katalog der Möglichkeiten zu gestalten?

Der interessante Punkt ist, dass dies genau das ist, was Familien tun, in denen Bildung ohne Schulbesuch stattfindet. Was sie tun, ist meist nicht ganz so formalisiert wie im obigen Beispiel, aber tatsächlich neigen diese Familien dazu, ihre eigenen Bildungsprogramme zu gestalten; sie suchen überall nach Elementen, die sie darin einbauen können, und viele der oben erwähnten Bausteine tauchen dabei auf. Aber ich wünsche mir, dass dieser Ansatz jedem Menschen im Rahmen des Bildungssystems zugänglich ist. Um dies zu erreichen, müssen wir die Schulen, wie wir sie kennen, schließen. Wir müssen ihr Personal, ihre Gebäude und ihre Ausstattung in ein gemeinschaftliches, auf freiwilliger Teilnahme beruhendes Bildungssystem umwandeln.

Meine Kontakte mit vielen Lehrern lassen mich vermuten, dass sie die Umstellung auf ein solches System *sehr begrüßen* würden. Tatsächlich sind, nach einer kürzlich von „City and Guilds Survey" erstellten Erhebung, die am 25. Februar 2005 in „*The Guardian*" veröffentlicht wurde, nur 8% von ihnen in dem derzeitigen System zufrieden; das heißt, 92% von ihnen wären für eine bessere Vision zu haben! *„Zeigt uns eine Vision, auf die wir stolz sein können und in der wir uns einbringen können, dann werden wir die Funktion von Experten haben, statt der von Mechanikern, die kleine Wissensstücke in Menschen einhämmern!"* Ich vermute, in einem solchen Bildungssystem werden die Lerner ihren Bildungsprozess selbst leiten und, mit Unterstützung und Führung, ihre eigene Wahl treffen.

Über Wahlmöglichkeiten gibt es eine Menge zu sagen; im derzeitigen System handelt es sich bei genauer Betrachtung um eine Wahlmöglichkeit der Art „Friss oder stirb!" – man hat eine eingeschränkte Auswahl unter einzelnen Dingen, die einem übergestülpt werden sollen. Eine echte Auswahl müsste sehr viel offener sein. Ich schlage ein personalisiertes Bildungssystem vor. Die Nutzung eines solchen Systems könnte uns in eine neue, aufregende, lebendige Bildungslandschaft führen – einer wahren Demokratie angemessen, auf der Grundlage von Wahlmöglichkeiten und -gelegenheiten!

Es stellten sich Fragen, die beantwortet wurden:

Einige Eltern, deren Kinder sich von zuhause aus bilden möchten, ermöglichen dies nicht, weil sie den Nutzen einer Ganztagsarbeit, das Geld, wollen. Wie können wir ihre Ansichten ändern, sie von unserem Standpunkt überzeugen?

Als erstes möchte ich hierauf antworten, dass alles, was im jetzigen System zur Verfügung steht, auch weiterhin zur Verfügung stehen könnte, aber es stünde zur freiwilligen Teilnahme zur Verfügung, nicht verpflichtend. Wenn also eine Familie meint: "hören Sie, wir haben das durchgesprochen, und es würde, zumindest für das kommende Jahr, unseren Bedürfnissen entsprechen, wenn wir Ihr Angebot fünf Tage die Woche von 9 Uhr bis 14 Uhr nutzen könnten; wir haben uns Ihr Programm angesehen und haben etwas gefunden, das wir machen wollen, und wir wären glücklich, wenn Sie in dieser Zeit unsere Kinder beaufsichtigen könnten; auf diese Art könnten wir unser Leben leben ", und wenn hiermit den Ansprüchen der Familie genügt wird, dann wird die Familie dieses Modell wählen. Aber es ist entscheidend, dass die Familie es auswählt und es nicht vom

Lernzentrum aufgezwungen wird. Das heißt, wenn eine Familie dieses Modell, welches zurzeit für diese Familie passend ist, nutzen möchte, dann wird sie sich dafür entscheiden.

Wird sie sich dann fortwährend wieder und wieder und wieder für dasselbe Modell entscheiden? Es gibt hier einen Hoffnungsschimmer in Form eines Modells in Amerika, das „year round education" („Bildung das ganze Jahr über") genannt wird. Eine ansehnliche Zahl von Schulen beteiligt sich an diesem Modell, das sich so entwickelt hat, dass das ganze Jahr hindurch ein Programm angeboten wird, täglich von acht Uhr morgens bis acht Uhr abends mit Ausnahme von Weihnachten. Im Rahmen dieses Modells wird Eltern eine Reihe von Pauschalangeboten gemacht. Sommerferienpakete, Wochenendpakete, Werktagspakete, Sommerpakete, Winterpakete. Aus diesem Programm kann sich jeder das Pauschalangebot auswählen, das für ihn brauchbar ist. Als dieses System in amerikanischen Schulen eingeführt wurde, war es zuerst so, dass die Mehrheit der Familien bei dem blieb, an das sie gewöhnt waren. Sie meinten: „Vielen Dank für die vielen Angebote, aber wir möchten gerne bei dem bleiben, was wir gewöhnt sind: am Montag kommen, bis Freitag arbeiten und dann Pause. Und wir möchten bei den üblichen Unterrichtsabschnitten bleiben, Sommerferien machen und danach wiederkommen, wenn es Ihnen recht ist." In Ordnung; wenn Sie sich dafür entschieden haben; Sie wissen, was man unter einem Angebot versteht. Etwa 10% der Eltern meinten: „Nein, können wir eines der anderen Modelle ausprobieren? Wir möchten gerne zu einem anderen Zeitpunkt Urlaub machen, wir hätten gerne im Winter Ferien; wir möchten die Wochenendkurse machen und unter der Woche pausieren." Es gab eine Gruppe von Vorreitern, welche das neue Modell ausprobierten. Und bei diesem Angebot der „Bildung das ganze Jahr über" in Teilen der USA, es existiert nicht überall in den USA, wurde festgestellt, dass im zweiten Jahr die 10% zu 20% wurden, im dritten Jahr waren es 40%, im vierten Jahr hatten mehr als die Hälfte der Menschen begonnen, die Vorteile der Wahlmöglichkeit zu nutzen. Ich denke daher, dass Hoffnung besteht – wenn man den Menschen Angebote macht, könnten sie zunächst zögerlich sein, aber wenn sie sehen, was andere Menschen daraus machen, werden sie wiederum denken: „Das will ich auch."

Es handelt sich um einen Vertrag, daher gibt es festgelegte Pauschalangebote, aber diese können ausgehandelt werden. Beispielsweise könnte es heißen: Wir bieten diesen Kurs in dieser Form an, aber wenn Sie eine andere Version wollen, können wir darüber verhandeln. Die Familien schließen den Vertrag. Es ist nicht die Zentralregierung, die festlegt: „So wird es gemacht." Es ist ein Angebot; wenn man sich entscheidet, eine Sache zu lassen, aber eine andere Sache zu tun und einen entsprechenden Vertrag abschließt, ist es in Ordnung.

Auch für Prüfungen gilt in einem zukünftigen Bildungssystem, dass sie ein Angebot darstellen. Als Modell schwebt mir hier die Offene Universität („Open University") vor. Dort werden Kurse abgehalten, an denen man teilnehmen kann, aber nach eigener Wahl kann man an diesen Kursen nur zum Vergnügen, ohne Bewertungen, teilnehmen, oder man kann den Kurs besuchen und zur eigenen Genugtuung an einigen der Bewertungen teilnehmen ohne ein Zeugnis zu bekommen, oder man kann an den vom Anbieter festgesetzten Bewertungen teilnehmen und ein Zeugnis erhalten. In gewissem Sinne ist die Offene Universität schon ein Stück dieses Weges vorangegangen, indem der Lerner entscheidet, wie viele Bewertungen er zu einem bestimmten Gebiet haben möchte, und wenn er gar keine will, dann heißt es: „in Ordnung, dann mach es einfach nur zum Vergnügen."

Prüfungen schränken das Lernen ein, aber mir scheint, dass es rechtfertigende Gründe für diese Einschränkung des Lernens gibt. Entscheidend ist, dass die Wahl vom Lerner ausgeht, das heißt, dass man selbst das Angebot ausgewählt hat, welches die Prüfungen und das Zeugnis umfasst. Ich möchte ein Beispiel aus dem Alltag anführen: Ich möchte nicht, dass jemand ohne entsprechendes Zeugnis an meinen Zähnen bohrt. Ich möchte, dass jemand die Ausbildung macht und sagt: „Ich wollte Zahnarzt werden, ich habe die Ausbildung gemacht, ich habe die Prüfungen bestanden und sie können Vertrauen in meine Arbeit haben." Hier hat ein Zeugnis eine Funktion. Aber es ist ein Fehler, dies der ganzen Bevölkerung aufzuerlegen. „**Jeder** muss eine Prüfung in Spanisch machen." „Warum? Für diejenigen, die eine Spanischprüfung machen wollen, wunderbar! Aber warum es allen aufzwingen?"

Mehr Informationen über gemeinschaftliche Lernzentren gibt es in einem in Amerika veröffentlichten Buch mit dem Titel „Creating Learning Communities" (www.creatinglearningcommunities.org/ resources/usa.htm), in dem Beispiele aus aller Welt angeführt werden. Sie sind ein bisschen mager, aber ich denke es gibt Beispiele gemeinschaftlicher Lernzentren und möglicherweise eines der besten sind ohne Schulbesuch lernende Menschen, die zusammenkommen um Lerngemeinschaften aufzubauen. Ähnlich wie die Gruppe auf der Isle of Wight, die die „Learning Zone" („Lerngebiet") aufbaute. Dort betreiben vierzig Familien ein gemeinschaftliches Lernzentrum. Sie definieren es, sie bringen ihre Wünsche ein, schauen sich das entstandene Programm an und entscheiden sich jeweils dafür, mitzumachen oder auszusteigen. Die Organisationsform der gemeinschaftlichen Lernzentren finden wir also in der Bildung ohne Schulbesuch selbst, aber ebenso in anderen Bereichen wie kommunalen Kunstprogrammen, wo es genauso gemacht wird. Grundsätzlich sieht ein gemeinschaftliches Lernzentrum im Wesentlichen aus wie eine Schule oder eine öffentliche Bibliothek, aber es lädt die Menschen ein, seine Möglichkeiten zu nutzen und zwingt sie nicht dazu. Sobald man anfängt, Angebote auf freiwilliger Basis einzuführen, beginnt man auch, das System zu wandeln.

What Home Educating Parents Can Teach the World about the Nature of Learning

by Dr. Alan Thomas
Visiting Fellow Institute of Education, University of London

Why Did I Become Interested in Informal Learning?
The story of how I became interested in informal learning mirrors what home educating parents go through.

I had felt there was something not quite right about my own schooling. Originally, the research I wanted to do was into what children actually learn in the classroom. My gut feeling was that schooling was totally inefficient, that children spend a lot of time learning very little. At the back of my mind all the time was the question, "What is it that is wrong with the way children learn in school?"

An advantage of teaching in a university was that I had the freedom to research what I wanted. So I thought, "Well, how do children learn? Let's look right back to classical times to see what philosophers and other educational thinkers had to say about children's learning. Across more than two millennia, what they nearly all said was that the best way to 'teach' children was individually. The upshot of this was an article called 'Individualized Teaching' (1992, *Individualised Teaching*, Oxford Review of Education, No 18)

In essence the obvious idea is that in order to teach efficiently you must discover what each child knows and how s/he thinks so that you can lead them on. Even in modern times educators talking about the best way of teaching children refer to individualized teaching. The interests of the individual are paramount. It simply doesn't make sense to teach thirty at the same time. You can't individualize in the classroom. But the rhetoric of classroom teaching is that this is exactly what you do. When parents go along to a school they can look at the brochures, which say 'we aim to educate your child in relating to your child's personal interests and needs'. This is something schools just cannot do.

I was working in Australia at this time and returned for a year to England where I went to see Roland Meighan. I was proud of my article on *Individualised Teaching* but I was a bit bemused to hear him say to someone else as I entered the room: "Ahhh, that Alan Thomas has got this thing about *teaching*." I thought, why say it like that? What's wrong with that then? After talking for a time he showed me a letter he had just received from a home educator saying, 'would anyone like to spend a week with us living in to see what it's like?' Thanks to him I am here today.

I spent a week with that home educating family. The first morning I was down early. I had breakfast, went upstairs, cleaned my teeth, came back down again and sat down with my clipboard. What happened next? Nothing happened. Half an hour later, still nothing happened. And then this boy came past me with a book in front of him, reading the book, and totally ignored me. And that's how the week continued. By the end if you had asked me to document what I'd seen in the way of teaching I would have said, "Not very much." I offered to teach the children probability and the Mother very politely said, "Well, maybe later in the week." And on Friday morning she said "Maybe this afternoon." In the afternoon she said, "Well now it's too late. It's not worth you starting." Very gently she'd pushed me out of teaching.

But on Wednesday a chance event happened. They were sitting round the table in the kitchen doing projects that were of interest to them. The mother was there cooking and I was sitting there with my clipboard and the conversation ranged from the political to "Can we have sticky buns for tea?" All sorts of topics came up. I thought, "Wow! This is learning through social conversation." There were little nuggets of learning in there! Nobody knew it; they all simply accepted it somehow.

The next article I wrote was called 'Conversational Learning' (1994 *Conversational Learning*, Oxford Review of Education, No 20, p.131-142) Again, you can't do this in a school because you don't have social conversation in a school. You have peer/peer conversation but you don't have social conversation with somebody who knows more than you. The teacher/pupil relationship is very set in its ways. At the end of the article I said the only way to find out more is through studying children who are home educated. I went back to a book that I had dismissed before; a wonderful book

by Barbara Tizard called *Young Children Learning at Home and in School.*
(Tizard, B. & Hughes, M (1984) London, Fontana.)

The book studied children who were half time nursery and half time at home, a standard thing in the British education system. They wanted to see what their language was like at home and in school. What they expected was a big class difference; that if you were middle class the level of language would be better at home, and if you're working class the level would be better than in school. But what they found astounded them. Anybody: working class or middle class, the level of language used between children and parents at home was of a far higher standard than that used in school. Not only was it of a higher standard but also the children themselves were able to follow their own logical means of enquiry. For example one child pursued his own understanding of Father Christmas and it is hard to work out if you're trying to be logical. It's following an argument through, 'how can – if': 'how can you do this, if that'.

Whereas in school the typical example they give is when a child walks up to a teacher with a piece of paper and says, "Can you cut it in half for me please?" and the teacher thinks 'Aha! Here's a teaching opportunity!' So she says "Go and get the scissors then." And the child gets them. By now the teacher has been distracted by a lot of things and then says, "Now what am I doing now? I am cutting it in …, what am I doing to this piece of paper?" "You're cutting it." The child says. "Yes, but what am I cutting it into, in two pieces, so what am I cutting it in?" The child says "You're cutting it for me into two pieces." This goes on for a bit until the teacher says, "I'm cutting it in *half.*" That child had asked the question "Can you cut it in half for me please?" There is a totally different quality of language between the two.

I went out to interview home educators. This was early in the 1990s. This was quite difficult at the time, as there was a lot of resistance to anyone coming from the outside who, 'might dob you in to the authorities'. What started as a very small-scale research project blossomed into a study of a hundred families based in Australia and in England. I found a very wide range of approaches from extremely formal, (one family rang a bell at 9am and the children came in from the garden for the lessons to start,) to the other extreme where the children did what they wanted with no apparent structure whatsoever.

In the beginning, when I had about 20 families in England, I gave a paper at a psychological conference where my listeners could be divided into those who were genuinely interested to those who thought that home education should not be allowed. On returning to Australia, I had a phone call from somebody in Tasmania who said, "Would you like to come and do some research?" I asked how he knew about me, and he said "You were in the paper the other day." I went down to the state library and looked up the local paper, 'The Hobart Mercury' and couldn't find any reference to me anywhere. Then I looked at the 'World News' and there it was – "Academic Says Home Education Works!"

Eventually I got a total of a hundred families taking part in my research. I found a few who carefully stuck to a school approach, a majority doing some structured work in the mornings leaving the rest of the day free and a small number who were completely and utterly informal, doing what the Americans call 'unschooling,' sometimes known in Britain as 'autonomous,' and in Australia as 'natural learning'. I would not for a moment say one approach is better than another. Perhaps the best advice, commonly given to new home educators who are unsure of themselves is to start with a structured approach and adapt as you go along.

However, I got interested in informal learning because I think formal learning at home isn't a big deal. A lot of professional educators think just taking a child out of the school system is a massive undertaking, but it's not really. There is no reason why anyone can't take a child through a textbook, if they are determined to. Informal learning is in a different category altogether. I was especially interested in those parents who had started formally and had gradually become informal because they are the ones who are discovering it for themselves and were not accepting any ideology.

How Do Parents Become Informal Home Educators?
There are two influences: first, the gradual realisation that school at home doesn't work. You don't need a timetable. These families had started with for example, planned lessons, and then learned it was not necessary. You just carry on from where you were before. Lesson planning, curriculum planning and timetables just aren't needed at all even if you stay fairly formal. There is no point in giving exercises because if you can do something, you can do it. There is no need to prove it over and over again. There is no need for marking or assessment because you know exactly where your child is up to. The beauty of it is the interactive element. Because you always know where your child is at, you're not wasting any time and it's highly intensive.

51

That's getting informal already by official educational standards but it goes further than this because the parents realised that their children were learning a lot outside the formal system. Because it was so intensive, most parents came to restrict teaching or structured learning to an hour or two in the morning. They came to realise that children were learning a lot outside this time without being taught. Phrases like, "I don't know where he got that from, he just knows it," or even "We do a course in maths but more maths seems to happen."

The second very important influence was from the children themselves. These are children who resist formal learning. At first this was terrible for the families. Parents told me that they were prepared to teach a very interesting lesson and the children resisted learning in this way; their eyes would become glazed, they weren't interested! Now, there is a significant difference here between school and home. In school you don't have all the children listening all the time, but you can't just say, 'well we'll stop there and do what you want for an hour'. You have to continue to teach the lesson regardless of who is listening or not listening. But at home, the feedback that you get is acute and the parents find it is pointless to keep teaching in this way. If you ally this with the observation that these children are learning anyway outside the formal system then there is a move away from formal learning. Some parents abandoned formal teaching altogether as a result. This is fascinating and leads to the title of my talk; "what home educating parents can teach the world about the nature of learning".

In schools and with professional educators everything comes directly from the adult, whereas home educators with children learning informally say that children learn a lot for themselves using the parent indirectly as a very important resource. This pointedly challenges establishment wisdom and educational theory.

Literacy
A brief word on literacy; I was not expecting literacy to feature too much in my research but what I found was surprising. Parents were telling me that their children had learnt to read at anything from the ages of 2 to 11. I thought it was odd. I've seen in other studies that some children learn to read late without any apparent drawback. In fact, because children in this country are forced to learn to read, whether they like it or not, whether they're interested or not, you get a rise in the standard of literacy in schools. It's like saying that if you swim 3 hours a day then there will be a rise in swimming ability and in the same way if

you go on and on about literacy it increases. However, this other research then showed that those children whose level of literacy had increased were less likely to read for pleasure. In my research when the children learned late, (say they are not reading at nine and then they start reading,) it was said to be 'like being on a downhill train'! Within 6 months or a year they are reading at an adult level. So when they are ready they will learn and they enjoy it.

How Do We Understand Informal Learning?

There are some people who have researched adult informal learning who describe it as 'elusive,' 'evanescent,' 'implicit' and very, very difficult to get hold of. Learning without knowing you're learning is very hard to document. How many people know how their children learnt to talk? They learn to talk. You see them learning sometimes and you get glimpses into the learning process but, first of all, they are not taught. Informal learning is very difficult to pin down.

I was very lucky in the first book I wrote to meet one parent who became obsessed with keeping a document of all her child's informal learning. I have a pile of exercise books to prove it! Over a period of time I spent weeks with this family when I was doing my research in Tasmania. Of course, relying on informal learning can be a bit scary. As the child's mother put it: "I don't know where it's all going. There are threads going here and threads going there and threads that don't seem to be going anywhere. I don't understand what's happening! I really feel sometimes I want to say, "right let's get that text book out and let's get on with some proper learning!" But she didn't and the child continued to learn. In fact, this child learned everything except what her mother tried to teach her, which was the multiplication tables, and this was when she was ten or eleven. But she did learn her 20 times table before any of the others because she found out that you could get money from supermarket trolleys. At the time this was 20 cents so when she was only about 5 or 6 years old, she knew her twenty times table. The motivation was there to learn. By the age of 11 she was on a par with what children in school had learned, so this completely informal approach to math does work.

So, trying to understand informal learning is difficult. You have all these little bits and pieces picked up from here and there. How on earth does a child in their brain, or me or you, put them all together into what becomes a coherent body of knowledge?

It seems there is informal learning, which is implicit; things you pick up without knowing you are picking them up. People sometimes say, "I don't know how I know that but I know it" and often it may be quite profound. Then there is informal learning which is goal directed for example a child spurred to find out about Roman life after seeing a film. There is a world of difference between this kind of learning and being taught it as part of a curriculum in school.

Current Research Article into Informal Education

At this point I decided to write an article on informal learning to try to pull together anything I could to understand it. To that end I have been collaborating with an anthropologist, Harriet Pattison, and we have just completed an academic article in which we explore informal learning theoretically and in depth. This was also partly in response to an Irish home educator who said that he feared the authorities would *never* understand informal learning.

So we looked across the board and there is some very interesting research into adult informal learning. One piece is with people in professions. The researchers wanted to know what informal learning had contributed to the advancement of professional knowledge. The problem was that the professionals (doctors, lawyers, social workers etc) didn't know what the researchers were talking about. The researchers had to explain what informal learning was. The upshot was that some of these; lawyers, medical specialists, came to understand that they were picking up a large amount in what one described as 'dribs and drabs' without knowing they were learning it, just by being around with colleagues (Garrick, J. (1998) *Informal Learning in the Workplace: Unmasking Human Resource Development.* London, Routledge)

I will quote from one if I may. This is a lawyer: "All through my career I have been engaged in informal learning without being aware of it; what your researchers call informal learning. Until you actually sit down and think about it you don't realise how much you actually do. It's not something you give any thought to at the time you are doing it, it just seems to happen in dribs and drabs. If I come across something I haven't come across before I can just ask a colleague because he has been around. Obviously, you can't sit all day chatting to people, but it is important to have exchanges with people, have room for that, not just the work things – and sometimes you might get a little bit of extra out of them that you never expected."(Gear, J., McIntosh, A. & Squires, G. (1994)

Informal Learning in the Professions. Department of Adult Education, University of Hull.)

A lot of research into informal learning is related to work. People go into a new job and they pick up a lot of their information informally. There is some research that shows people learn more efficiently informally than if they have specific little courses designed to teach certain skills. A good example of this is a study with Brazilian carpenters who, without ever having been on a course, have a better understanding of maths related to carpentry than do apprentices who have just finished a taught course teaching the same material. That kind of informal learning must be good – because you don't even know you are doing it! These people are simply learning alongside others who are better at it than they are and they gradually pick it up (Carraher, D.W. & Schliemann, A.D. (2000) Reasoning in mathematics education: realism versus meaningfulness, in: D.H. Jonassen & S. M. Land (Eds) *Theoretical Foundations of Learning Environments.* New Jersey, Lawrence Earlbaum Associates)

So we then looked at early learning. We all know that you cannot *teach* infants to talk, but there is very little research into informal early learning because it is assumed by the educators that, even with very young children, it is always adult led; that any learning, which is of any use, must come from the adult, maybe fairly informally, but the adult sets the agenda. What this article re-enforces, however, is the pro-active nature of informal learning. Children will learn what they need to. Children will learn what they need to in the culture that they are in. In other words, as somebody said, "we are predisposed to learn our culture". Now if that culture includes intellectual elements: basic maths, being articulate, learning to read, then this knowledge will be acquired.

How do children learn to read informally? Well, there are words around you all the time. There are shop names, street names, and you see adults reading. It is something that you do in the culture and because it is part of what you do in the culture you are interested in doing it; hence children of three or four will pretend to write because it is a cultural skill they want to acquire. Another thing is that parents read to children, and many children just 'learn to read.' Not all, of course, some have problems, but a lot just seem to learn to read without being 'taught'. This is really shocking to a professional educator! In fact the chief inspector of schools for Ofsted [central government's Office for Standards in Education] said, and I quote "the idea that children could learn to read by osmosis is plain crackers." ("Teaching in 1960s crackers, says inspector" in: Rebecca Smithers The Guardian , Wednesday October 6, 2004). Now that really riles me because you have somebody here who is supposed to be well educated himself, but he is not willing even to think of anything else; he just goes along with one simple ideology without allowing for any other possibilities!

We made an interesting finding when looking at learning through play such as happens in Nursery schools for example. There is a debate in this country between the 'free flow' play people and the educational 'managers' who say that no play is worth anything unless it is properly managed with educational objectives within the play. And yet it was observed that if you simply leave children to play, "within minutes of being given props children are creating detailed and sustained play activities and in these activities they recreate the world they experience. They cook, they clean, they polish, they plan, they travel, they explore, they fall ill, they are hospitalised and recover, they teach, they scold, they punish, they fall in love, they get married and have children. There is hardly any area of life that can't be found in children's play! The way we interpreted this is that, again, it is part of the culture. Play is a way to practice being in the culture." (Hall, N. (1994) Play, Literacy and the role of the teacher, J. R. Moyles (Ed.) in: *The Excellence of Play.* Philadelphia, Open University Press) Overall, therefore, what is coming out of this article is that informal learning is characterised by a desire on the part of the child to learn the culture. This is not to learn the culture in order to be in the culture – the child is in the culture from the start. Someone has described this as being like a club, the child is a member of that club and therefore it is assumed s/he will gradually acquire adult ways of behaving, adult values and attitudes *and* intellectual knowledge that is integral to the culture.

Learning through play is accepted for young children. We know that children continue to learn through play after they have reached school age, and yet in schools it is looked upon as a waste of time and of recreational value only. However, there are countless examples of children learning and trying out quite complex things through play.

How Do Children Learn Informally?
How do they learn on a minute-by-minute level? One way is through observation – by watching what people do. There was a lovely advert on the TV in Australia aiming to cut down on alcoholic consumption. It showed two little children acting like their parents. The Mother was in the house and the

Father came in saying 'oh, I've had a hard day!' and this little kid of three or four went straight to the fridge pretending to get his beer and drink it. So the little girl said 'Well I'll have a glass of wine' and the caption was 'Everything you do they are watching … and learning!' We all use observation as a way to learn and so do young children.

Another way of learning we came across was practice. You may think, 'oh no, that sounds boring; it's what children in school do!' but we found that children learning informally, they do a lot of practice. There was one little girl being educated informally and we were in the car once when, out of the blue she said, 'in six years time I'll be thirteen' and her mother said, 'that's good, how did you work that out?' and the little girl replied, 'I always do add ups and take always in my head.' She was practicing. She wasn't being told to; it was just an informal thing to do, and this was how she was able to refine and extend her mathematical knowledge.

Another way of learning we observed was 'intellectual search.' Tizard and Hughes (*Young Children Learning at Home and in School. 1984* London, Fontana) use this phrase in their research. When they are very young children ask questions all the time; following a logical train of thought either on their own or with parents or whatever. As children grow older this seems to be extended. I have found in my research and in follow up research I am doing, that older children who are educated at home informally are able to follow something as far as they would like. One boy studied only chemistry for a year. This is advanced intellectual search.

However we still don't know how, from all these little bits and pieces of knowledge and without realising it, children come to 'know' in informal learning. There might be elements of teaching such as when a child asks something and you tell them, you can call that an element of teaching, but it is very different from a parent saying 'Right, I am going to teach you something now.'

Conclusions
So what do we conclude from all this? Two things; firstly, in so far as intellectual skills and knowledge are part and parcel of the culture, they can be acquired without being separated from all the social things that people are doing, simply as a part of growing up. The best parallel is learning to talk.

Children learn the grammar of their language, which is very complex, without any teaching at all.

Secondly, the kind of learning that is going on during the first few years can be extended beyond early childhood and through to the later years. Professional educators cannot see this. Suddenly there is a cut off and children are exposed to a totally different kind of pedagogy. The first pedagogy is pro-active and informal. The second is 'I will tell you what to learn.' They are very, very different.

Follow-up Research
Just as a taste of some follow up research, currently, Harriet Pattison and I are writing a follow up to my first book.. Most of the parents, no matter how formal or informal they were, now say that they could have been a little bit more informal, or they wish they had been more informal. That is a general finding no matter what else the parents say. There is a variety of outcomes. Some of the children do extremely well; top university entrance scores etc. Some are more middle of the road. What they all seem to have, is an idea of where they want to go. For example, somebody reaches 'A' level, or the equivalent, and you ask what university they are going to. They might say, 'I don't know. I don't think I will go actually.' They have learned to be responsible for themselves and to make their own decisions.

Ce que les parents qui instruisent à la maison peuvent enseigner au monde sur la nature de l'apprentissage

par Dr Alan Thomas
Visiting Fellow, (Chercheur en résidence), Institute of Education, Université de Londres

Pourquoi me suis-je intéressé à l'apprentissage informel ?
La manière dont je me suis intéressé à l'apprentissage informel reflète le chemin que parcourent les parents qui instruisent à la maison.

J'avais le sentiment qu'il y avait quelque chose qui clochait dans ma propre scolarité. À l'origine, l'étude que je voulais effectuer concernait ce que les enfants apprennent véritablement en classe. Mon sentiment profond était que l'école est totalement inefficace, les enfants y passant beaucoup de temps pour apprendre très peu de choses. En arrière-plan, j'avais tout le temps à l'esprit la question : « Qu'est-ce qui ne va pas dans la manière dont les enfants apprennent à l'école ? ».

L'avantage d'enseigner à l'université est que j'avais la liberté de choisir mon thème de recherche. Alors j'ai pensé : « Bon, comment les enfants apprennent-ils ? Regardons en arrière, ce que les philosophes et autres penseurs en éducation de l'époque classique avaient à dire sur l'apprentissage des enfants. » Sur plus de 2000 ans, ce qu'ils disaient presque tous, c'est que le meilleur moyen d'instruire un enfant c'est individuellement. Le résultat de ce travail a été un article intitulé : *L'enseignement individualisé* (1992, « Individualised Teaching », *Oxford Review of Education*, N° 18).

En essence, l'idée évidente est que pour enseigner efficacement, on doit découvrir ce que chaque enfant sait et comment il/elle pense, afin de pouvoir le/la guider. Même à l'époque moderne, les éducateurs qui parlent du meilleur moyen d'instruire des enfants se réfèrent à l'enseignement individualisé. L'intérêt de l'individu est souverain. Cela n'a tout simplement aucun sens d'enseigner à trente à la fois. On ne peut pas individualiser en classe. Or, l'institution scolaire clame le contraire, et les parents qui se rendent dans une école peuvent lire des brochures qui disent : « Notre objectif est d'instruire votre enfant en fonction de ses intérêts et de ses besoins personnels ». C'est là quelque chose que les écoles ne peuvent tout simplement pas faire.

Je travaillais en Australie à cette époque, et je suis retourné un an en Angleterre, où je suis allé rencontrer Roland Meighan. J'étais fier de mon article sur « L'enseignement individualisé », mais j'ai été assez stupéfié de l'entendre dire à quelqu'un d'autre alors que j'entrais dans la pièce : « Ahhh, cet Alan Thomas a écrit ce truc sur *l'enseignement* ». J'ai pensé : « Pourquoi dit-il cela ? Qu'est-ce qui ne va pas ? » Après avoir discuté un certain temps, il m'a montré une lettre qu'il venait juste de recevoir d'une personne qui instruisait ses enfants à la maison et qui disait : « Est-ce que quelqu'un voudrait passer une semaine à vivre avec nous, pour voir comment nous faisons ? ». C'est grâce à lui que je suis ici aujourd'hui.

J'ai passé une semaine avec cette famille qui faisait l'instruction à la maison. Le premier matin, je me suis levé tôt. J'ai pris mon petit déjeuner, je suis remonté me laver les dents, et suis redescendu m'asseoir avec mon carnet de notes. Que s'est-il passé ensuite ? Rien. Une demi-heure plus tard, toujours rien. Puis ce garçon est passé devant moi, en lisant un livre tout en marchant, et il m'a complètement ignoré. Et la semaine a continué de la même manière. A la fin, si l'on m'avait demandé de décrire ce que j'avais vu en matière d'enseignement, j'aurais répondu : « pas grand chose ». J'ai proposé d'enseigner les probabilités aux enfants, et la mère m'a répondu très poliment : « Eh bien, peut-être plus tard dans la semaine. » Et le vendredi matin elle m'a dit : « Peut-être cet après-midi. » Et l'après-midi elle m'a dit : « C'est trop tard maintenant, ce n'est pas la peine que vous commenciez. » Très délicatement, elle m'avait écarté de l'enseignement.

Mais le mercredi, il se passa par hasard un événement. Ils étaient assis autour de la table de la cuisine à faire des choses qui les intéressaient. La mère faisait la cuisine et j'étais assis avec mon carnet de notes, et la conversation allait de la politique à « est-ce qu'on peut avoir des petits pains au lait au goûter ? ». Toutes sortes de sujets sont venus. J'ai pensé : « Waouh ! C'est de l'apprentissage au travers de la conversation sociale ». Il y avait de petites pépites d'apprentissage là-dedans ! Personne n'y pensait ; ils l'acceptaient tous simplement.

L'article suivant que j'ai écrit s'intitulait « L'apprentissage par la conversation » (1994 « Conversational Learning », *Oxford Review of Education*, N° 20, p.131-142). Une fois de plus, ce n'est pas quelque chose que l'on peut faire dans une école, parce qu'il n'y a pas de conversation sociale à l'école. Il y a des discussions entre pairs, mais pas avec quelqu'un qui en sait plus que vous. La relation enseignant / élève est très figée à sa manière. A la fin de l'article, je disais que le seul moyen d'en savoir plus était d'étudier les enfants instruits à la maison. Je suis revenu à un livre que j'avais écarté jusqu'alors, un merveilleux livre de Barbara Tizard intitulé *L'apprentissage des jeunes enfants à la maison et à l'école* (*Young Children Learning at Home and in School*. 1984, Tizard, B. & Hughes, M, Londres, Fontana).

Les auteurs étudiaient des enfants qui étaient à mi-temps à la maternelle et à mi-temps à la maison, ce qui est très courant dans le système éducatif britannique. Ils voulaient savoir comment était leur langage à la maison et à l'école. Ce à quoi ils s'attendaient était à une grande différence selon la classe sociale : ceux qui étaient de classe moyenne auraient eu un meilleur niveau de langage à la maison, et ceux de la classe ouvrière à l'école. Mais ce qu'ils ont trouvé les a surpris : toutes les familles, qu'elles soient de la classe ouvrière ou de la classe moyenne, utilisaient à la maison entre parents et enfants un niveau de langage nettement supérieur à celui utilisé à l'école. Non seulement le niveau était supérieur, mais les enfants étaient même capables de suivre leur propre logique d'enquête. Par exemple, un enfant essayait de se faire sa propre idée du Père Noël, et ce n'est pas facile puisqu'il. faut recourir à un raisonnement du type « si..., alors comment... » : « comment peut-on faire ceci, si cela ? ».

À l'école, en revanche, l'exemple typique que l'on donne de la démarche enseignante est celui d'un enfant qui va vers l'enseignante avec une feuille de papier et qui dit : « Pouvez-vous me la couper en deux moitiés s'il vous plaît ? » et l'enseignante de penser « Ah, voici une occasion d'enseigner ! » et de répondre : « Va me chercher des ciseaux ». L'enfant va les chercher. Entre-temps, l'enseignante a été distraite par une multitude de choses et dit : « Alors qu'est-ce que je dois faire déjà ? Je dois la couper en..., qu'est-ce que je fais avec cette feuille ? ». « Vous la coupez », dit l'enfant. « Oui, mais comment est-ce que je la coupe ? En deux, donc qu'est-ce que ça fait ? ». L'enfant répond : « Vous la coupez en deux pour moi ». Ca continue un moment comme ça jusqu'à ce que l'enseignante dise : « Je la coupe en deux *moitiés* ». C'est ce que l'enfant avait dit dès le début. Il y a une qualité de langage totalement différente entre les deux.

Je suis allé interroger des parents qui enseignent à la maison. C'était au début des années 90. C'était assez difficile en ce temps-là, parce qu'il y avait beaucoup de réticence à laisser venir quelqu'un de l'extérieur qui pouvait vous dénoncer aux autorités. Ce qui a commencé comme un projet de recherche à très petite échelle a pris les dimensions d'une étude de centaines de familles basées en Australie et en Angleterre. J'ai trouvé une très grande variété d'approches, allant d'une démarche extrêmement formelle (une famille faisait sonner la cloche à 9h et les enfants rentraient du jardin pour commencer les leçons) à l'autre extrême, où les enfants faisaient ce qu'ils voulaient sans quelque structure apparente que ce soit.

Au début, quand je suivais une vingtaine de familles en Angleterre, j'ai fait une intervention dans un colloque en psychologie, où l'on trouvait parmi les participants aussi bien ceux qui étaient véritablement intéressés que ceux qui pensaient que l'instruction à la maison ne devrait pas être autorisée par la loi. De retour en Australie, j'ai eu un appel d'une personne en Tasmanie qui m'a dit : « Seriez-vous intéressé à venir faire une étude ici ? ». Je lui ai demandé comment il me connaissait et il m'a répondu : « Vous étiez dans le journal l'autre jour ». Je suis allé à la bibliothèque centrale consulter le journal local, The Hobart Mercury, et je n'y ai trouvé aucune référence me concernant. Puis j'ai regardé les Nouvelles du Monde et j'ai trouvé : « Un universitaire dit que l'instruction à la maison marche ! ».

Finalement, je me suis retrouvé avec une centaine de familles participant à mon étude. J'en ai trouvé quelques unes qui restaient soigneusement collées à une approche scolaire, une majorité qui faisait du travail structuré le matin et le reste de la journée restait libre, et un petit nombre qui avait une pratique complètement et résolument informelle, faisant ce que les Américains appellent unschooling (« non-scolarisation »), quelquefois connu en Angleterre sous le terme d'apprentissage autonome et en Australie sous celui d'apprentissage naturel. Je n'aurais pas dit qu'une approche était meilleure que les autres. Peut-être que le meilleur conseil que l'on donne souvent aux parents qui se lancent dans l'instruction en famille et qui ne sont pas très sûrs d'eux, c'est de commencer avec une approche structurée et de s'adapter au fur et à mesure.

Cependant, je me suis intéressé à l'apprentissage informel parce que je pense que l'apprentissage formel à la maison ne mérite pas qu'on en fasse toute une histoire. Beaucoup d'éducateurs professionnels pensent que sortir un enfant du système scolaire est en soi une grande entreprise, mais ce n'est pas le cas. Il n'y a aucune raison qui empêche quiconque de faire suivre un manuel scolaire à un enfant, s'il y est déterminé. L'apprentissage informel appartient à une tout autre catégorie. J'étais particulièrement intéressé par les parents qui avaient commencé formellement et étaient peu à peu devenus informels, parce que ce sont ceux qui découvrent par eux-mêmes et qui n'acceptent aucune idéologie.

Comment les parents qui instruisent leurs enfants deviennent-ils des éducateurs informels ?
Il y a deux influences : d'abord, la constatation graduelle que l'école à la maison ne marche pas. Il n'y a pas besoin d'un emploi du temps. Ces familles avaient commencé, par exemple, avec des leçons planifiées, et puis elles avaient compris que ce n'était pas nécessaire. C'est juste parce qu'on continue sur sa lancée. Planifier les leçons et le programme, avoir un emploi du temps, ce n'est tout simplement pas nécessaire même si l'on reste plutôt formel. Il ne sert à rien de donner des exercices, parce que si l'on sait faire quelque chose, on sait le faire. Il n'y a pas besoin de le prouver encore et encore. Il n'y a pas besoin d'évaluation parce que l'on sait exactement où en est notre enfant. Le bon côté réside dans l'élément interactif. Parce que l'on sait toujours où en est notre enfant, on ne perd pas de temps et c'est très intensif.

C'est déjà devenir informel selon les standards officiels d'éducation, mais cela va plus loin parce que les parents ont réalisé que leurs enfants apprenaient beaucoup en dehors du système formel. Comme c'était très intensif, beaucoup de parents en sont arrivés à restreindre l'enseignement ou l'apprentissage structuré à une heure ou deux le matin. Ils en sont venus à réaliser que les enfants apprenaient beaucoup en dehors de ce temps, sans qu'on leur enseigne, comme en témoignent des phrases telles que : « Je ne sais pas où il a pris ça, mais il le sait », ou même « On suit un cours de maths mais il semble qu'il apprenne plus que le cours ».

La seconde influence très importante est venue des enfants eux-mêmes. Ce sont des enfants qui résistent à l'apprentissage formel. Au début, c'était terrible pour les familles. Les parents me racontaient qu'ils s'étaient préparés à enseigner une leçon très intéressante, et les enfants résistaient à apprendre de cette manière; leur regard devenait vide, ils n'étaient pas intéressés ! Là, il y a une différence significative entre l'école et la maison. A l'école, tous les enfants n'écoutent pas tout le temps, mais on ne peut pas se permettre de dire : « Bon, on va s'arrêter là et faire ce que tu veux pendant une heure ». On doit continuer le cours, qu'ils écoutent ou non. Mais à la maison, le feedback que l'on obtient est direct, et les parents trouvent qu'il est sans intérêt de continuer à enseigner de cette manière. Si l'on ajoute cela à l'observation que ces enfants apprennent de toutes façons en dehors du système formel, alors il y a tendance à s'écarter de l'apprentissage formel. En résultat, certains parents ont finalement complètement abandonné l'enseignement formel. C'est fascinant, et c'est ce qui conduit au titre de mon exposé : « Ce que les parents qui instruisent à la maison peuvent enseigner au monde sur la nature de l'apprentissage ».

Dans les écoles et avec les éducateurs professionnels, tout vient directement de l'adulte, alors que les parents qui instruisent informellement à la maison disent que les enfants apprennent beaucoup par eux-mêmes en utilisant indirectement les parents comme une ressource très importante. Cela remet en question de manière aiguë les idées établies de l'institution et les théories de l'éducation.

La lecture
Un petit mot sur la lecture: je ne m'attendais pas à ce que la lecture occupe trop de place dans mon étude, mais ce que j'ai trouvé était surprenant. Les parents me disaient que leurs enfants avaient appris à lire à tout âge entre 2 et 11 ans. J'ai trouvé cela étrange. J'ai vu dans d'autres études que certains enfants apprennent à lire tard sans aucun inconvénient apparent. En fait, comme dans ce pays les enfants sont forcés d'apprendre à lire qu'ils le veuillent ou non, qu'ils soient intéressés ou non, on obtient un accroissement du standard de lecture dans les écoles. Cela revient à dire que si l'on nage trois heures par jour alors il y a un accroissement de la capacité à nager, et, de la même manière, si l'on insiste sur la lecture, le niveau augmente. Mais ces autres études montrent que ces enfants scolarisés dont le niveau de lecture s'est élevé, sont moins susceptibles de lire pour le plaisir. Dans mes recherches, lorsque les enfants lisaient tardivement, (disons qu'ils ne lisent pas à 9 ans et qu'ils commencent à lire à ce moment), c'était comme de prendre un TGV ! En six mois ou un an, ils lisent comme un adulte. Donc, quand ils sont prêts, ils apprennent et ça leur plaît.

Que comprenons-nous de l'apprentissage informel ?
Certaines personnes qui ont étudié l'apprentissage informel des adultes le décrivent comme 'insaisissable', 'évanescent', 'implicite', et très, très difficile

à mettre en évidence. Apprendre sans savoir que l'on apprend est très difficile à décrire. Combien de personnes savent comment leurs enfants ont appris à parler ? Ils apprennent à parler, point. On les voit apprendre quelquefois, et l'on a des aperçus du processus d'apprentissage, mais, avant tout, personne ne le leur enseigne. L'apprentissage informel est très difficile à cerner.

J'ai eu la grande chance lorsque j'écrivais mon premier livre de rencontrer une mère qui avait l'obsession de garder la trace écrite de tous les apprentissages informels de son enfant. J'ai une pile de cahiers pour le prouver ! Pendant un temps, j'ai passé des semaines dans cette famille quand je faisais mon étude en Tasmanie. Bien sûr, il peut être un peu effrayant de se reposer sur l'apprentissage informel. Comme le disait la mère de cette enfant : « Je ne sais pas où cela mènera. Il y a des éléments qui vont dans un sens et des éléments qui vont dans un autre et des éléments qui semblent aller nulle part. Je ne comprends pas ce qui se passe ! J'ai parfois le sentiment que je voudrais dire : "Allez, on prend ce manuel et on fait du vrai apprentissage !" ». Mais elle ne l'a pas fait et l'enfant a continué à apprendre. En fait, cette enfant apprenait tout sauf ce que sa mère avait essayé de lui enseigner, à savoir les tables de multiplication, quand elle avait dix ou onze ans. Mais elle avait appris la table de 20 avant toutes les autres parce qu'elle avait trouvé que l'on pouvait avoir de l'argent avec les caddies de supermarché. A cette époque c'était 20 centimes, donc quand elle avait seulement 5 ou 6 ans, elle connaissait la table de 20. La motivation pour apprendre était là. A l'âge de 11 ans, elle était au niveau de ce que les enfants apprennent à l'école, donc cette approche complètement informelle des maths fonctionne.

Il est donc difficile d'essayer de comprendre l'apprentissage informel. Il y a tous ces différents petits morceaux pêchés ici ou là. Comment diable le cerveau des enfants, ou le mien ou le vôtre, met-il tous ces morceaux ensemble dans ce qui devient une connaissance cohérente ?

Il semble qu'il y ait deux modes d'apprentissage informel : un mode implicite dans lequel on récolte des choses sans savoir qu'on les récolte. Les gens disent parfois : « Je ne sais pas comment je sais ça, mais je le sais » et souvent cela peut être assez approfondi. Et puis, il y a l'apprentissage informel dirigé vers un but, comme c'est le cas de l'enfant désireux de connaître la vie des Romains après avoir vu un film. Il y a un monde entre ce type d'apprentissage et apprendre quelque chose parce que c'est au programme à l'école.

Mon dernier article de recherche sur l'instruction informelle
J'ai alors décidé d'écrire un article sur l'apprentissage informel pour essayer de réunir tout ce que je pouvais en comprendre. Pour cela, j'ai collaboré avec une anthropologiste, Harriet Pattison, et nous venons de terminer un article académique dans lequel nous explorons l'apprentissage informel du point de vue théorique en profondeur. C'était aussi en partie pour répondre à un parent irlandais instruisant à la maison, qui disait qu'il craignait que les autorités ne puissent *jamais* comprendre l'apprentissage informel.

Nous avons donc regardé un peu plus loin et trouvé des études très intéressantes sur l'apprentissage informel des adultes. L'une d'elles concerne les professions libérales (Garrick, J. (1998), *L'apprentissage informel au travail : démasquer le développement des Ressources Humaines – Informal Learning in the Workplace : Unmasking Human Resource Development,*. Londres, Routledge). Les chercheurs voulaient savoir quels apprentissages informels avaient contribué à faire avancer les connaissances dans ces domaines. Le problème était que les personnes concernées (médecins, juristes, travailleurs sociaux…) ne comprenaient pas de quoi les chercheurs parlaient. Les chercheurs devaient expliquer ce qu'était l'apprentissage informel. Le résultat a été que certains d'entre eux (juristes, spécialistes médicaux…) en sont venus à comprendre qu'ils récoltaient beaucoup d'informations dans ce que l'un d'eux décrivait comme un 'compte-gouttes', sans savoir qu'ils apprenaient, juste en étant avec des collègues.

Je vais citer l'un d'eux si je puis me permettre. C'est un juriste: « Tout au long de ma carrière j'ai été engagé dans de l'apprentissage informel sans en être conscient – ce que vos chercheurs appellent *apprentissage informel*. Tant que vous ne prenez pas le temps d'y réfléchir, vous ne réalisez pas tout ce que vous faites. Ce n'est pas quelque chose à quoi vous accordez la moindre pensée au moment où vous le faites, ça semble juste arriver au compte-gouttes. Si je tombe sur quelque chose que je n'avais pas rencontré auparavant, je peux juste demander à un collègue parce qu'il est dans le coin. Bien évidemment, vous ne pouvez pas passer toute la journée à discuter, mais c'est important d'avoir des échanges avec les gens, d'avoir de la place pour cela, pas seulement pour les choses professionnelles – et quelquefois il peut en ressortir quelque chose de complètement inattendu ». (Gear, J., McIntosh, A. & Squires, G. (1994) *L'apprentissage informel dans les professions libérales – Informal Learning in the Professions.* Département de Formation des Adultes, Université de Hull.)

De nombreuses études dans le domaine de l'apprentissage informel sont liées au travail. Les gens commencent un nouveau travail et ils récoltent une grande partie des informations de manière informelle. Certaines études montrent que les gens apprennent plus efficacement de manière informelle que s'ils suivent de petites formations spécifiques pour enseigner certaines compétences. Un bon exemple en est une étude sur des menuisiers brésiliens qui, sans jamais avoir eu de formation, ont une meilleure compréhension des mathématiques en rapport avec la menuiserie que des apprentis qui viennent de sortir d'une formation sur le même sujet (Carraher, D.W. & Schliemann, A.D. (2000), « Reasoning in mathematics education : realism versus meaningfulness », in : D.H. Jonassen & S. M. Land (Eds) *Les fondations théoriques des environnements d'apprentissage – Theoretical Foundations of Learning Environments*. New Jersey, Lawrence Earlbaum Associates). Ce genre d'apprentissage informel doit être bon – parce que vous ne savez même pas que vous le faites ! Ces gens apprennent simplement à côté d'autres qui en savent plus qu'eux, et ils accumulent peu à peu ce savoir.

Nous avons alors regardé les premiers apprentissages. Nous savons tous que l'on ne peut pas *enseigner* aux bébés à parler, mais il y a très peu d'études sur les premiers apprentissages informels parce qu'il est communément admis par les éducateurs que, même avec les très jeunes enfants, c'est toujours organisé par les adultes ; que tout apprentissage qui ait une quelconque utilité doit provenir de l'adulte : même s'il se fait de façon informelle, c'est l'adulte qui définit l'ordre du jour. Alors que ce sur quoi cet article insiste, c'est sur la nature proactive de l'apprentissage informel. Les enfants vont apprendre ce qu'ils ont besoin d'apprendre. Ils vont apprendre ce qu'ils ont besoin d'apprendre dans la culture dans laquelle ils sont. En d'autres termes, comme le disait quelqu'un, « nous sommes prédisposés à apprendre notre culture ». Donc, si cette culture comprend des éléments intellectuels (mathématiques de base, savoir bien s'exprimer, apprendre à lire), alors ces connaissances s'acquerront.

Comment les enfants apprennent-ils à lire informellement ? Eh bien, il y a des mots autour de nous en permanence. Il y a les noms des magasins, des rues, et l'on voit les adultes lire. C'est quelque chose que l'on fait dans la culture et parce que cela fait partie de ce que l'on fait dans la culture, c'est intéressant de le faire ; ainsi les enfants de trois-quatre ans vont faire semblant d'écrire parce que c'est une compétence culturelle qu'ils veulent acquérir. Un autre point est que les parents font la lecture aux enfants, et beaucoup d'enfants apprennent à lire juste de cette façon. Pas tous, bien sûr, certains ont des difficultés, mais beaucoup semblent apprendre à lire sans qu'on le leur « enseigne ». C'est vraiment choquant pour un éducateur professionnel ! En fait, l'Inspecteur Principal des écoles de l'Ofsted (le Bureau central du gouvernement pour les Normes d'Education) a dit, je cite : « L'idée que les enfants pourraient apprendre à lire par osmose est du pipeau » (Rebecca Smithers, « L'inspecteur dit que l'enseignement des années soixante est du pipeau », *The Guardian*, mercredi 6 octobre 2004). Cela m'exaspère vraiment, parce que c'est quelqu'un qui est supposé avoir lui-même une bonne éducation, mais il ne veut même pas penser qu'il puisse en être autrement ; il se contente d'une idéologie simple sans permettre aucune autre possibilité !

Nous avons fait une découverte intéressante en observant l'apprentissage par le jeu, tel qu'il se passe en Maternelle par exemple. Il y a un débat dans mon pays entre les partisans du « jeu libre » et les « organisateurs éducatifs » qui disent qu'aucun jeu n'a de valeur s'il n'est pas organisé correctement avec des objectifs éducatifs inclus dans le jeu. Et pourtant, on observe que si on laisse simplement des enfants jouer, « dans les minutes qui suivent, les enfants créent des jeux précis et durables et dans ces jeux ils recréent le monde dont ils font l'expérience : ils cuisinent, ils nettoient, ils astiquent, ils font des plans, ils voyagent, ils explorent, ils tombent malades, ils sont hospitalisés et guérissent, ils enseignent, ils grondent, ils punissent, ils tombent amoureux, se marient et ont des enfants. Il n'y a pratiquement aucun domaine de la vie qui échappe aux jeux des enfants ! La manière dont nous l'avons interprété est que, encore une fois, cela fait partie de la culture. Le jeu est un moyen de s'exercer à être dans la culture » (Hall, N. (1994), « Play, Literacy and the role of the teacher", in : J. R. Moyles (Ed.), *L'excellence du jeu – The Excellence of Play*. Philadelphie, Open University Press). Il ressort donc globalement de cet article que l'apprentissage informel se caractérise par le désir de la part de l'enfant d'apprendre la culture. Ce n'est pas apprendre la culture afin d'en faire partie – l'enfant en fait partie dès le début. Quelqu'un a décrit cela comme un club, l'enfant appartient à ce club et on s'attend donc à ce qu'il/elle acquière graduellement les manières de se comporter des adultes, les valeurs et les attitudes des adultes *et* les connaissances intellectuelles qui font partie intégrante de cette culture.

L'apprentissage par le jeu est accepté pour les jeunes enfants. Mais nous savons que les enfants continuent d'apprendre par le jeu après avoir atteint l'âge scolaire, et pourtant, dans les écoles, le jeu est considéré comme une perte de temps et comme n'ayant pas d'autre valeur que récréative. Cependant, il y a d'innombrables exemples d'enfants apprenant et s'essayant à des choses très complexes grâce au jeu.

Comment les enfants apprennent-ils de manière informelle ?
Comment apprennent-ils instant après instant ? L'une des modalités de ce type d'apprentissage est l'observation – en regardant ce que font les gens. Il y avait une charmante publicité à la télévision en Australie dont l'objectif était de diminuer la consommation d'alcool. Elle montrait deux petits enfants imitant leurs parents. La mère était à la maison et le père rentrait en disant : « Oh, j'ai eu une journée terrible ! », et ces deux petits enfants de trois ou quatre ans allaient tout droit au réfrigérateur et faisaient semblant de prendre une bière et de la boire. La petite fille disait alors : « Bon, je vais prendre un verre de vin », et le message était : « Tout ce que vous faites, ils le regardent... et ils l'apprennent ! » Nous utilisons tous l'observation comme moyen d'apprendre, et les jeunes enfants aussi.

Un autre moyen d'apprentissage que nous avons rencontré passe par la pratique. Vous pensez peut-être : « Oh non, ce n'est pas intéressant, c'est ce que font les enfants à l'école ! », mais nous avons trouvé que les enfants qui apprennent de manière informelle s'entraînent beaucoup. Il y avait une petite fille qui était instruite de manière informelle et alors que nous étions en voiture, elle a dit tout à coup : « Dans six ans, j'aurai treize ans » et sa mère a répondu : « C'est vrai, comment as-tu trouvé ça ? » et la petite fille a répondu : « J'ajoute et j'enlève tout le temps dans ma tête ». Elle s'entraînait. On ne lui disait pas de le faire ; c'était juste une chose informelle qu'elle faisait, et c'est par ce moyen qu'elle pouvait approfondir et développer ses connaissances mathématiques.

Une autre manière d'apprendre que nous avons observée est la « recherche intellectuelle ». Tizard et Hughes (*L'apprentissage des jeunes enfants à l'école et à la maison*, 1984, Londres, Fontana) utilisent cette expression dans leur étude. Quand ils sont très jeunes, les enfants posent tout le temps des questions ; ils suivent une logique de pensée, soit par eux-mêmes, soit avec leurs parents ou quiconque autour d'eux. Quand les enfants grandissent, il semble que cela s'amplifie. J'ai trouvé lors de cette étude et de l'étude suivante que je mène actuellement que des enfants plus grands instruits informellement à la maison sont capables de poursuivre quelque chose aussi loin qu'ils le désirent. Un garçon n'a étudié que la chimie pendant un an. C'est de la recherche intellectuelle avancée.

Pourtant, nous ne savons toujours pas comment, dans l'apprentissage informel, à partir de tous ces petits éléments de connaissances et sans s'en rendre compte, les enfants en arrivent à « savoir ». Il peut y avoir des éléments d'enseignement, comme lorsqu'un enfant pose une question et qu'on lui répond ; on peut appeler cela un élément d'enseignement, mais c'est très différent d'un parent qui dirait : « Bon, maintenant je vais t'apprendre quelque chose. »

Conclusions

Que peut-on donc conclure de tout ceci ? Deux choses : premièrement, dans la mesure où des capacités intellectuelles et des connaissances font partie intégrante de la culture, elles peuvent être acquises sans être séparées de tout ce que les gens font socialement, par le fait de grandir tout simplement. Le meilleur parallèle que l'on puisse faire est l'apprentissage de la parole. Les enfants apprennent la grammaire de leur langue, qui est très complexe, sans qu'on leur enseigne quoi que ce soit.

Deuxièmement, le mode d'apprentissage des toutes premières années peut être étendu au-delà de la petite enfance, jusqu'à n'importe quel âge. Les éducateurs professionnels ne peuvent pas s'en rendre compte. Brusquement, il y a une coupure et les enfants sont exposés à un mode pédagogique complètement différent. La première pédagogie est proactive et informelle. La deuxième est fondée sur le « je vais te dire ce que tu vas apprendre ». Elles sont très, très différentes.

Recherches en cours

Juste pour vous donner un aperçu des recherches qui ont suivi, nous sommes actuellement, Harriet Pattison et moi, en train d'écrire une suite à mon premier livre. La plupart des parents, qu'ils aient été plutôt formels ou informels, disent maintenant qu'ils auraient pu être un peu plus informels, ou regrettent de ne pas avoir été plus informels. C'est une conclusion générale, quoi que les parents disent par ailleurs. Les résultats sont très variés. Certains enfants s'en sortent extrêmement bien : meilleurs résultats d'entrée à l'université, etc. D'autres sont plus moyens. Ce qu'ils semblent tous avoir, c'est une idée de ce qu'ils veulent. Par exemple, quelqu'un a une mention TB ou quelque chose d'équivalent, et vous lui demandez à quelle université il va aller. Il peut répondre : « Je ne sais pas. En fait, je ne crois pas que je vais y aller. » Ils ont appris à être responsables d'eux-mêmes et à prendre leurs propres décisions.

Was zu Hause unterrichtende Eltern der Welt über das Wesen des Lernens beibringen können

Von Dr. Alan Thomas

Gaststipendiat am Institut für Erziehungswissenschaft, Universität London
(Visiting Fellow, Institute of Education, University of London)

Woher rührt mein Interesse an informellem Lernen?

Die Geschichte, wie ich ein Interesse an informellem Lernen entwickelte, spiegelt wider, was Familien durchmachen, bei denen Bildung von zu Hause aus stattfindet.

Ich hatte das Gefühl, dass etwas mit meiner eigenen schulischen Bildung nicht ganz in Ordnung war. Ursprünglich wollte ich Nachforschungen darüber anstellen, was Kinder im Klassenzimmer eigentlich lernen. Mein Bauchgefühl sagte mir, dass schulische Bildung total ineffizient sei, dass Kinder viel Zeit damit verbringen, sehr wenig zu lernen. In meinem Hinterkopf stellte sich immer die Frage, „Was stimmt nicht an der Art, wie Kinder in der Schule lernen?"

Da ich an der Universität lehrte, hatte ich den Vorteil, meinen Forschungsbereich frei wählen zu können. So dachte ich, „Nun, wie lernen Kinder eigentlich?" Lassen Sie uns zurückblicken in das klassische Zeitalter, um zu sehen, was Philosophen und andere pädagogische Denker über das Lernen von Kindern zu sagen hatten. Was fast alle von ihnen, über mehr als zwei Jahrtausende hinweg, sagten, war, dass es am Besten sei, die Kinder individuell zu „unterrichten". Das Ergebnis dieser Nachforschung war ein Artikel mit dem Titel „Individualisierter Unterricht" (1992, *Individualised Teaching*, Oxford Review of Education, No 18)

Im Wesentlichen ist die naheliegende Idee die, dass man, um effizient unterrichten zu können, entdecken muss, was jedes einzelne Kind weiß und wie es denkt, so dass man es führen kann. Sogar in modernen Zeiten verweisen Pädagogen auf Einzelunterricht, wenn sie über die beste Art des Unterrichts reden. Die Interessen des Einzelnen sind vorrangig. Es macht einfach keinen Sinn, dreißig zur gleichen Zeit zu unterrichten. Man kann im Klassenzimmer nicht individualisieren. Aber die Behauptung zum Unterricht im Klassenzimmer ist, dass genau das gemacht wird. Wenn Eltern ihre Kinder zur Schule begleiten, können sie Broschüren anschauen, in denen steht „unser Ziel ist es, Ihr Kind entsprechend seinen persönlichen Interessen und Bedürfnissen zu unterrichten." Das ist etwas, was Schulen einfach nicht leisten können.

Zu dieser Zeit arbeitete ich in Australien und kehrte für ein Jahr nach England zurück, wo ich Roland Meighan besuchte. Ich war stolz auf meinen Artikel *„Individualized Teaching"* aber ich war ein bisschen irritiert, als ich ins Zimmer kam und ihn zu jemandem anderen sagen hörte: „Ahhh, dieser Alan Thomas hat diesen Fimmel mit dem **Unterrichten**." Ich dachte, warum sagt er das so? Was ist denn so falsch daran? Nachdem wir uns ein wenig unterhalten hatten, zeigte er mir einen Brief, den er gerade von jemandem erhalten hatte, dessen Kinder sich von zu Hause aus bilden. Darin stand: „würde jemand gerne eine Woche bei uns wohnen, um zu sehen, wie das ist?" Dank ihm bin ich heute hier.

Ich verbrachte eine Woche mit dieser von zu Hause aus lernenden Familie. Am ersten Morgen war ich früh unten. Ich frühstückte, ging nach oben, putzte die Zähne, kam wieder nach unten und setzte mich mit meinem Klemmbrett in der Hand hin. Was geschah als nächstes? Nichts geschah. Nach einer halben Stunde geschah noch immer nichts. Und dann lief ein Junge an mir vorbei mit einem Buch vor der Nase. Er las und ignorierte mich vollständig. Und so ging es die Woche über weiter. Und am Ende, wenn man mich gebeten hätte zu dokumentieren, was ich an Unterricht gesehen hätte, hätte ich geantwortet, „Nicht sehr viel." Ich bot an, den Kindern Wahrscheinlichkeitsrechnung beizubringen, und die Mutter antwortete sehr höflich, „Nun, vielleicht später die Woche." Und am Freitag morgen sagte sie, „Vielleicht heute Nachmittag." Am Nachmittag sagte sie, „Nun, jetzt ist es zu spät. Es lohnt sich nicht, jetzt noch anzufangen." Sehr sanft hat sie mich vom Unterrichten abgehalten.

Aber am Mittwoch ereignete sich etwas Zufälliges. Sie saßen in der Küche um den Tisch und gingen Projekten nach, die sie interessierten. Die Mutter kochte und ich saß da mit meinem Klemmbrett. Die Unterhaltung reichte vom Politischen bis zu „Können wir Sticky Buns zum Tee haben?" Alle möglichen Themen kamen auf den Tisch. Ich dachte, „Wow! Das ist Lernen durch soziale Unterhaltung." Da waren kleine Brocken Lernen dabei! Niemand wusste das; irgendwie hatten alle das einfach akzeptiert.

Der nächste Artikel, den ich schrieb, hieß "Lernen durch Konversation" (1994 *Conversational Learning*, Oxford Review of Education, No 20, p.131-142). Das ist noch etwas, was an einer Schule nicht stattfinden kann, weil man an der Schule keine sozialen Unterhaltungen führt. Dort gibt es Unterhaltungen mit Altersgenossen, aber keine sozialen Unterhaltungen mit jemandem, der mehr weiß als man selbst. Das Lehrer/Schüler-Verhältnis ist sehr eingefahren. Am Ende des Artikels erklärte ich, dass man nur durch Studien über Kinder, die ohne Schule leben und lernen, mehr erfahren kann. Ich griff zurück auf ein Buch, das ich zuvor abgetan hatte; ein wundervolles Buch von Barbara Tizard mit dem Titel *Young Children Learning at Home and in School.* (Tizard, B. & Hughes, M (1984) London, Fontana.)

In diesem Buch beschäftigen sich die Autoren mit Kindern, die die Hälfte ihrer Zeit in der Kinderkrippe, die andere Hälfte zu Hause verbrachten, eine sehr gängige Situation im britischen Bildungssystem. Sie wollten die Sprache der Kinder zu Hause und in der Schule untersuchen. Sie erwarteten einen großen Klassenunterschied; dass, wenn man zur Mittelklasse gehört, das Niveau der Sprache zu Hause besser ist, und wenn man zur Arbeiterklasse gehört, das Niveau der Sprache in der Schule besser ist. Aber was sie vorfanden, erstaunte sie. Bei allen, egal ob Arbeiterklasse oder Mittelklasse, war das Niveau der Sprache, die zwischen Eltern und Kindern zu Hause benutzt wurde, weitaus höher als das der in der Schule benutzten Sprache. Es handelte sich nicht nur um ein höheres Sprachniveau; die Kinder waren auch selbst in der Lage ihre eigenen logischen Überlegungen und Gedankengänge zu verfolgen. Ein Kind zum Beispiel verfolgte sein eigenes Verständnis vom Weihnachtsmann, und das ist schwierig zu erarbeiten, wenn man versucht, logisch vorzugehen. Es ist die Durchführung eines Arguments, „wie kann ..., wenn ..."; „Wie kann man dies machen, wenn das ...".

Das Beispiel, das die Autoren als für die Schule typisch anführen, sieht hingegen folgendermaßen aus: Ein Kind geht mit einem Stück Papier zur Lehrerin und sagt, „Können Sie das bitte für mich in zwei Hälften schneiden?" und die Lehrerin denkt, „Aha! Hier habe ich die Gelegenheit, etwas zu unterrichten!" Und so sagt sie „Dann geh und hole die Schere." Und das Kind holt sie. In der Zwischenzeit ist die Lehrerin von vielen Dingen abgelenkt worden und sagt dann, „Nun, was tue ich jetzt? Ich schneide es in... Was mache ich mit diesem Stück Papier?" „Sie schneiden es.", sagt das Kind. „Ja, aber in was schneide ich es, in zwei Stücke, also in was schneide ich es?" Das Kind sagt, „Sie schneiden es für mich in zwei Stücke." Das geht eine Weile weiter bis die Lehrerin sagt,

„Ich schneide es in *zwei Hälften*." Das Kind hatte die Frage gestellt: „Können Sie das bitte für mich in zwei Hälften schneiden?" Die Sprachqualität ist in den beiden Situationen völlig unterschiedlich.

Ich zog los, um Familien zu interviewen, in denen Bildung ohne Schulbesuch stattfindet. Das war in den frühen 90er Jahren. Zu der Zeit war das sehr schwierig, weil es sehr viel Argwohn gab gegenüber Leuten, die von außen kamen, und die „einen vielleicht an die Behörden verpfeifen". Was als Untersuchung in sehr kleinem Umfang begann, gedieh zu einer Studie mit hundert Familien aus Australien und England. Ich fand ein breites Spektrum von Ansätzen von extrem formal (in einer Familie wurde um 9 Uhr morgens eine Glocke geläutet und die Kinder kamen zum Beginn des Unterrichts vom Garten herein), bis hin zum anderen Extrem, wo die Kinder taten, was ihnen gefiel, ohne irgendwelche ersichtlichen Strukturen.

Anfangs, als ich ungefähr 20 Familien in England hatte, präsentierte ich eine Veröffentlichung bei einer Psychologiekonferenz, bei der meine Zuhörer in zwei Gruppen eingeteilt werden konnten: Die, die wirklich interessiert waren und die, die dachten, Lernen ohne Schule sollte nicht erlaubt sein. Als ich nach Australien zurückkam, erhielt ich einen Anruf von einem Mann aus Tasmanien, der mich fragte, „Hätten Sie Lust, hierher zu kommen und ihre Forschung hier weiter zu betreiben?" Ich fragte, wie er von mir gehört hatte, und er sagte, „Sie waren heute in der Zeitung." Ich ging zur Staatsbibliothek und schaute in die Lokalzeitung, „The Hobart Mercury", und konnte nirgends einen Hinweis auf mich finden. Dann schaute ich in die Rubrik „World News", die Weltnachrichten, und da war es – „Akademiker sagt: Lernen ohne Schule funktioniert!"

Im Endeffekt nahmen hundert Familien an meinen Nachforschungen teil. Ich fand darunter ein paar, die sich sehr sorgfältig an den schulischen Ansatz hielten, eine Mehrzahl, die morgens etwas strukturiert arbeiteten und den Nachmittag frei hielten, und eine kleine Anzahl, die absolut und völlig informell an die Sache herangingen, was die Amerikaner „unschooling" nennen und was in Großbritannien manchmal als „autonomes" und in Australien als „natürliches Lernen" bekannt ist. Ich würde mich nicht für einen Moment festlegen wollen, welcher dieser Ansätze besser ist als die anderen. Möglicherweise ist es der beste Ratschlag – der Familien, für die Bildung von zu Hause aus neu ist und die sich daher noch unsicher fühlen, üblicherweise gegeben wird – mit einem strukturierten Ansatz zu beginnen und ihn dann nach und nach anzupassen.

Ich jedenfalls begann mich für informelles Lernen zu interessieren, weil ich denke, formales Lernen zu Hause ist nichts Besonderes. Viele professionelle Pädagogen denken, dass es schon ein gewaltiges Unterfangen ist, wenn man ein Kind nur aus dem Schulsystem nimmt, aber das ist es nicht wirklich. Jeder kann mit einem Kind ein Schulbuch durcharbeiten, wenn er sich das vorgenommen hat. Informelles Lernen gehört in eine gänzlich andere Kategorie. Ich war besonders an denjenigen Eltern interessiert, die formal angefangen hatten und nach und nach informeller geworden sind, denn dies sind die Eltern, die das informelle Lernen selbst entdecken und nicht irgendeiner Ideologie folgen.

Wie kommen Eltern zur informellen Bildung ohne Schulbesuch?
Es gibt zwei Einflüsse: zum Einen die allmähliche Erkenntnis, dass Schule zu Hause nicht funktioniert. Man braucht keinen Stundenplan. Diese Familien begannen beispielsweise mit vorbereiteten Unterrichtsstunden und haben dann erfahren, dass diese unnötig sind. Man macht einfach immer da weiter, wo man vorher aufgehört hat. Unterrichtsplanung und das Aufstellen von Lehr- und Stundenplänen sind ganz einfach nicht nötig, selbst wenn man ziemlich formal bleibt. Übungen aufzugeben macht keinen Sinn, denn wenn man etwas kann, dann kann man es. Man braucht es nicht wieder und wieder unter Beweis zu stellen. Man braucht auch nicht zu benoten und zu bewerten, denn man weiß immer genau, wo sein Kind gerade steht. Das Schöne daran ist das Element der Gegenseitigkeit. Weil man immer weiß, wo sein Kind steht, verschwendet man keine Zeit und das Ganze ist hochintensiv.

Das ist, gemessen an den offiziellen Bildungsstandards, schon ziemlich informell, aber es geht noch weiter, weil die Eltern merkten, dass ihre Kinder sehr viel außerhalb des formalen Systems lernten. Weil es so intensiv war, beschränkten die meisten Eltern das Unterrichten oder strukturierte Lernen auf eine oder zwei Stunden am Morgen. Sie stellten fest, dass ihre Kinder außerhalb dieser Zeit eine Menge lernten, ohne unterrichtet zu werden. Sätze wie „ich weiß nicht, wo er das her hat, er weiß es einfach," oder sogar „Wir machen einen Mathekurs aber der größere Teil des Mathelernens scheint nebenbei stattzufinden."

Der zweite sehr wichtige Einfluss kam von den Kindern selbst. Das sind Kinder, die sich gegen das formale Lernen sträuben. Zuerst war das schrecklich für die Familien. Eltern erzählten mir, dass sie eine sehr interessante Unterrichtsstunde vorbereitet hatten und die Kinder sich dagegen gesträubt haben, auf diese Weise zu lernen; ihre Augen wurden glasig, sie waren nicht interessiert!

Nun, hier liegt ein entscheidender Unterschied zwischen Schule und Zuhause. In der Schule hören nicht immer alle Kinder zu, aber man kann nicht einfach sagen, „nun gut, wir hören hier auf und du kannst eine Stunde lang machen, was dir gefällt". Man muss weitermachen mit dem Unterricht, ohne Rücksicht darauf wer zuhört und wer nicht. Aber zu Hause ist die Rückmeldung die man bekommt unmissverständlich, und die Eltern finden es sinnlos, auf diese Art weiter zu unterrichten. Wenn man das mit der Beobachtung verbindet, dass diese Kinder außerhalb des formalen Systems sowieso lernen, dann ergibt sich eine Bewegung weg vom formalen Lernen. Einige Eltern haben demzufolge das formale Unterrichten komplett aufgegeben. Das ist faszinierend und bringt uns zum Titel meines Vortrags: „Was zu Hause unterrichtende Eltern der Welt über das Wesen des Lernens beibringen können."

In Schulen und bei professionellen Pädagogen kommt alles direkt vom Erwachsenen. Dahingegen erklären Familien mit Kindern, die von zu Hause aus auf informelle Weise lernen, dass Kinder eine Menge selbst lernen und dabei die Eltern indirekt als wichtige Quelle benutzen. Das stellt ganz direkt die allgemein akzeptierte Sichtweise und die Bildungstheorie in Frage.

Lese- und Schreibfähigkeit
Eine kurzes Wort zur Lese- und Schreibfähigkeit; ich hatte nicht erwartet, dass Lese- und Schreibfähigkeit in meinen Nachforschungen eine wichtige Rolle spielen würden, aber was ich fand war überraschend. Eltern erzählten mir, dass ihre Kinder irgendwann zwischen 2 und 11 Jahren lesen gelernt hatten. Ich fand das seltsam. Ich habe in anderen Studien gesehen, dass manche Kinder spät anfangen zu lesen ohne irgendwelche erkennbaren Beeinträchtigungen. Weil Kinder in diesem Land zum Lesenlernen gezwungen werden, ob sie nun wollen oder nicht, ob sie interessiert sind oder nicht, ist es tatsächlich so, dass dadurch das Niveau der Lesefähigkeit in Schulen ansteigt. Das ist so als sage man, wenn man 3 Stunden täglich schwimmt, dann steigt die Schwimmfähigkeit; und auf die gleiche Weise erhöht sich die Lesefähigkeit, wenn man damit immer weitermacht. Jedoch zeigten diese anderen Forschungen dann, dass es unwahrscheinlicher ist, dass diese Kinder, deren Lesefähigkeit anstieg, zum Vergnügen lesen. In meinen Forschungen wurde gesagt, wenn die Kinder spät zu lesen begannen (sagen wir, sie können mit neun Jahren noch nicht lesen und beginnen dann damit), dann war das, „als wäre man auf einem Zug, der bergab fährt"! Innerhalb von 6 Monaten oder einem Jahr lasen sie auf dem Niveau eines Erwachsenen. Wenn sie also bereit sind, dann lernen sie und es macht ihnen auch Spaß.

Wie verstehen wir informelles Lernen?

Es gibt Leute, die das informelle Lernen von Erwachsenen untersucht haben, und die es als „schwer fassbar", „dahinschwindend", „implizit" und sehr, sehr schwierig festzuhalten beschreiben. Es ist sehr schwer, Lernen zu dokumentieren von dem man nicht weiß, dass man es tut. Wie viele Menschen wissen, wie ihre Kinder sprechen gelernt haben? Sie lernen eben sprechen. Manchmal sieht man sie beim Lernen und man bekommt kleine Einblicke in den Lernprozess, aber sie werden nicht darin unterrichtet. Informelles Lernen ist sehr schwer zu greifen.

Ich hatte das große Glück, beim Schreiben meines ersten Buches eine Mutter kennen zu lernen, die davon besessen war, das ganze informelle Lernen ihres Kindes zu dokumentieren. Ich habe einen Stapel Hefte, die das belegen! Eine Zeit lang verbrachte ich ganze Wochen mit dieser Familie, als ich meinen Studien in Tasmanien nachging. Natürlich kann es einem ein bisschen Angst machen, wenn man auf informelles Lernen vertraut. Mit den Worten der Mutter: „Ich weiß nicht, wo all dies hinführt. Manche Fäden führen hier hin, andere Fäden führen dorthin und manche scheinen überhaupt nirgends hinzuführen. Ich verstehe nicht, was passiert! Manchmal ist mir danach zu sagen, 'so, jetzt holen wir das Lehrbuch raus und lernen mal anständig!'" Aber sie tat es nicht und das Kind lernte weiter. In der Tat lernte das Kind alles mit Ausnahme dessen, was ihre Mutter ihr beizubringen versuchte, nämlich das Einmaleins. Das war, als sie zehn oder elf war. Aber sie hat die 20er-Reihe vor allen anderen gelernt, weil sie herausgefunden hatte, dass man mit Hilfe der Einkaufswagen im Supermarkt Geld bekommen kann. Zu jener Zeit waren das 20 Cent, und so konnte sie mit gerade mal 5 oder 6 Jahren die 20er-Reihe. Die Motivation zum Lernen war gegeben. Mit 11 Jahren entsprach ihr Wissensstand dem, was Kinder in der Schule gelernt hatten. Dieser informelle Ansatz zu Mathe funktioniert also.

Der Versuch, informelles Lernen zu verstehen, ist also schwierig. Man hat all diese kleinen Brocken, die man hier und dort mitgenommen hat. Wie um alles in der Welt verbindet ein Kind, oder Sie oder ich, das alles in seinem Hirn zu einem zusammenhängenden Wissensbild?

Es scheint informelles Lernen zu geben, das unbewusst stattfindet; Dinge, die man einfach aufnimmt ohne zu wissen, dass man sie aufnimmt. Manchmal sagen Leute: „Ich weiß nicht, woher ich das weiß, aber ich weiß es" und oft sind das ziemlich tiefgründige Sachen. Und dann gibt es informelles Lernen, das zielorientiert ist. Ein Kind, zum Beispiel, das sich nach einem Film dazu angeregt fühlt, etwas über das Leben der alten Römer zu erfahren. Es liegen Welten zwischen dieser Art zu lernen und wenn man als Teil des Schullehrplans darin unterrichtet wird.

Aktueller Forschungsartikel über informelle Bildung

Zu diesem Zeitpunkt entschloss ich mich, einen Artikel über informelles Lernen zu schreiben, um zu versuchen, alles zusammentragen, was dabei helfen würde es zu verstehen. Um das zu erreichen, habe ich mit einer Anthropologin, Harriet Pattison, zusammengearbeitet, und wir haben gerade einen akademischen Artikel fertiggestellt, in dem wir das informelle Lernen auf theoretischer Ebene und tiefgehend ergründen. Dieser Artikel entstand teilweise auch als Antwort an ein irisches Elternteil, dessen Kinder sich ohne Schulbesuch bildeten. Er erklärte, er befürchte, die Behörden würden informelles Lernen *niemals* verstehen.

Also haben wir ganz allgemein gesucht und festgestellt, dass es einige sehr interessante Forschungen im Bereich des informellen Lernens bei Erwachsenen gibt. Eine Arbeit beschäftigt sich mit Menschen im Berufsleben. Die Forscher wollten herausfinden, was das informelle Lernen zur Förderung des fachlichen Wissens beigetragen hatte. Das Problem war nur, dass die Berufstätigen (ÄrztInnen, RechtsanwältInnen, SozialarbeiterInnen, etc), nicht wussten, wovon die Forscher sprachen. Die Forscher mussten erst erklären, was informelles Lernen ist. Das Ergebnis war, dass einigen - RechtsanwältInnen, medizinischen SpezialistInnen - bewusst wurde, dass sie eine große Menge, wie einer es beschrieb, „tröpfchenweise" aufschnappten, ohne zu wissen, dass sie es lernten, einfach nur, indem sie Zeit mit Kollegen verbrachten. (Garrick, J. (1998) *Informal Learning in the Workplace: Unmasking Human Resource Development.* London, Routledge)

Ich werde, wenn es gestattet ist, einen von ihnen zitieren. Es war ein Anwalt: „Während meiner ganzen Laufbahn war ich mit informellem Lernen beschäftigt ohne mir dessen bewusst zu sein; mit dem, was ihre Forscher informelles Lernen nennen. Bis man sich wirklich hinsetzt und darüber nachdenkt, merkt man gar nicht, wie viel davon eigentlich stattfindet. Es ist nichts, worüber man nachdenkt, während man es tut, es scheint einfach tröpfchenweise stattzufinden. Wenn mir etwas begegnet, was mir vorher noch nie begegnet ist, kann ich einfach einen Kollegen fragen, weil der mehr Erfahrung hat. Natürlich kann man nicht den ganzen Tag rumsitzen und sich mit Leuten unterhalten, aber es ist wichtig, sich mit Menschen auszutauschen, dem Raum zu geben, nicht nur für berufsbezogene Angelegenheiten - und manchmal bekommt man eine kleine Zugabe, die man niemals erwartet hätte." (Gear, J., McIntosh, A. & Squires, G. (1994) *Informal Learning in the Professions*. Department of Adult Education, University of Hull.)

Eine Menge Nachforschungen zum informellen Lernen beziehen sich auf das Arbeitsleben. Leute fangen eine neue Arbeit an und greifen viel ihrer Information informell auf. Es gibt ein paar Forschungen, die aufzeigen, dass Leute auf informelle Weise effizienter lernen, als wenn sie spezielle kleine Kurse besuchen, die bestimmte Fähigkeiten vermitteln sollen. Ein gutes Beispiel dafür ist eine Studie mit brasilianischen Zimmerleuten, die, ohne jemals einen Kurs besucht zu haben, ein besseres Verständnis von Mathe im Bezug auf Zimmermannsarbeiten hatten, als Lehrlinge, die gerade erst einen Kurs beendet hatten, in dem die gleiche Materie unterrichtet wurde. Diese Art informellen Lernens muss gut sein - denn man weiß nicht einmal, dass man es tut! Diese Leute lernen einfach an der Seite von Anderen, die darin besser sind, und sie schnappen es einfach nach und nach auf. (Carraher, D.W. & Schliemann, A.D. (2000) Reasoning in mathematics education: realism versus meaningfulness, in: D.H. Jonassen & S. M. Land (Eds) *Theoretical Foundations of Learning Environments*. New Jersey, Lawrence Earlbaum Associates.)

Dann betrachteten wir das Lernen in der frühen Kindheit. Wir wissen alle, dass man Babys nicht im Sprechen **unterrichten** kann, aber es gibt nur sehr wenige Forschungen über frühkindliches informelles Lernen, da die Pädagogen davon ausgehen, dass, selbst bei sehr jungen Kindern, das Lernen immer von Erwachsenen gesteuert ist; dass alles Lernen, was für irgendetwas nützlich ist, von einem Erwachsenen kommen muss, vielleicht auf ziemlich informelle Art und Weise, aber der Erwachsene gibt den Plan vor. Dieser Artikel bekräftigt aber das selbstgesteuerte Wesen des informellen Lernens. Kinder lernen, was sie brauchen. Kinder werden lernen, was sie in der Kultur, in der sie leben, brauchen. In anderen Worten, wie jemand einmal sagte, „wir sind darauf ausgerichtet, unsere Kultur zu lernen". Wenn diese Kultur nun intellektuelle Elemente beinhaltet – grundlegende Mathekenntnisse, sich gut artikulieren können, Lesen lernen – dann wird dieses Wissen erworben.

Wie lernen Kinder auf informelle Weise lesen? Nun, wir sind ständig von Wörtern umgeben. Es gibt die Namen von Läden, Straßennamen, und man sieht

Erwachsene lesen. Es ist etwas, was in der Kultur getan wird, und weil es etwas ist, was in der Kultur getan wird, ist man daran interessiert, es zu tun. Daher tun kleine Kinder von drei oder vier Jahren so, als können sie schreiben; weil es eine kulturelle Fähigkeit ist, die sie erwerben wollen. Eine weitere Sache ist, dass Eltern ihren Kindern vorlesen, und viele Kinder „lernen einfach lesen". Nicht alle, versteht sich, einige haben Probleme, aber viele scheinen das Lesen einfach zu lernen, ohne darin „unterrichtet" zu werden. Das ist wirklich schockierend für einen professionellen Pädagogen! Tatsächlich hat der leitende Schulinspektor des OFSTED (central government's Office for Standards in Education – zentrales Regierungsamt für Bildungsstandards in Großbritannien) erklärt, und ich zitiere, „die Vorstellung, dass Kinder das Lesen durch Osmose lernen können ist schlicht und einfach verrückt." ("Teaching in 1960s crackers, says inspector" in: Rebecca Smithers The Guardian , Wednesday October 6, 2004). So etwas ärgert mich wirklich, weil das jemand ist, der selbst gebildet sein sollte, aber er ist nicht bereit, etwas anderes auch nur zu denken; er schließt sich einfach einer simplen Ideologie an, ohne andere Möglichkeiten zuzulassen!

Wir haben eine interessante Entdeckung gemacht, als wir uns näher mit Lernen durch Spielen, wie zum Beispiel im Kindergarten, beschäftigten. In diesem Land gibt es eine Debatte zwischen den Befürwortern des freien Spiels und den „Bildungsmanagern", die behaupten, dass jegliches Spiel wertlos ist, das nicht ordentlich geleitet wird und keine Lernziele innerhalb des Spiels enthält. Und dennoch hat man beobachtet, dass Kinder, die einfach ihrem Spiel überlassen wurden, „innerhalb weniger Minuten, nachdem sie Requisiten zum Spielen erhalten haben, detaillierte und anhaltende Spielaktivitäten gestalten. Und in diesen Aktivitäten rekonstruieren sie die Welt, die sie erleben. Sie kochen, sie putzen, sie polieren, sie planen, sie reisen, sie erforschen, sie werden krank, sie werden ins Krankenhaus eingewiesen und erholen sich wieder, sie unterrichten, sie schimpfen, sie bestrafen, sie verlieben sich, sie heiraten und bekommen Kinder. Es gibt so gut wie keinen Lebensbereich, der im Kinderspiel nicht wiedergefunden werden kann! Wir interpretieren das wieder so, dass es Teil der Kultur ist. Spiel ist eine Möglichkeit, das Sein in der Kultur zu üben." (Hall, N. (1994) Play, Literacy and the role of the teacher, J. R. Moyles (Ed.) in: *The Excellence of Play.* Philadelphia, Open University Press) Was wir also im Großen und Ganzen dem Artikel entnehmen ist, dass informelles Lernen durch den Wunsch des Kindes geprägt ist, die Kultur zu erlernen. Das bedeutet nicht, die Kultur zu erlernen, um in der Kultur zu sein - das Kind ist von Anfang an in der Kultur. Jemand hat es so beschrieben, dass es wie ein Club ist. Das Kind ist ein

Mitglied des Clubs und deshalb wird davon ausgegangen, dass es sich nach und nach das Verhalten der Erwachsenen, die Werte und Einstellungen der Erwachsenen *und* das für die Kultur wesentliche intellektuelle Wissen aneignen wird.

Spielerisches Lernen wird bei kleinen Kindern allgemein akzeptiert. Wir wissen, dass Kinder auch nachdem sie das Schulalter erreicht haben, weiterhin spielerisch lernen, und doch wird es in Schulen als Zeitverschwendung angesehen. Lediglich Erholungswert wird ihm zugestanden. Und dennoch gibt es zahllose Beispiele von Kindern, die im Spiel recht komplizierte Dinge gelernt und ausprobiert haben.

Wie lernen Kinder auf informelle Art und Weise?
Wie lernen sie ganz konkret von Minute zu Minute? Zum Einen durch Beobachtung – indem sie zuschauen, was Menschen tun. In Australien gab es einen herrlichen Werbespot im Fernsehen, der darauf ausgerichtet war, Alkoholkonsum zu verringern. Gezeigt wurden zwei kleine Kinder, die so taten als seien sie ihre Eltern. Die Mutter war zu Hause, und der Vater kam herein mit den Worten „oh, was hatte ich für einen schweren Tag!" Und dieser kleine Junge von drei oder vier Jahren lief schnurstracks zum Kühlschrank und tat so als hole er sich sein Bier und tränke es. Und das kleine Mädchen sagte „Nun, ich werde mir ein Glas Wein genehmigen". Und die Bildunterschrift lautete „Sie sehen alles, was du tust ... und lernen es!" Wir alle benutzen Beobachtung als ein Mittel zum Lernen, und kleine Kinder tun es genauso!

Eine weiteres Lernverfahren, dem wir begegnet sind, war das Üben. Sie denken vielleicht, „oh nein, das klingt langweilig; das tun Kinder in der Schule!" Aber wir entdeckten, dass Kinder, die informell lernen, sehr viel üben. Ein kleines Mädchen, das auf informelle Weise lernte, war mit uns im Auto, und aus heiterem Himmel sagte sie, „in sechs Jahren bin ich dreizehn", und ihre Mutter sagte, „das ist richtig, wie hast du das herausbekommen?" und das kleine Mädchen antwortete, „Ich rechne immer plus und minus in meinem Kopf." Sie übte. Nicht, weil ihr jemand sagte, sie solle es tun. Es war einfach etwas Informelles, was sie tat, und auf diese Weise konnte sie ihr Mathematikverständnis verfeinern und erweitern.

Eine weitere Art zu lernen, die wir beobachteten, war die „intellektuelle Nachforschung" („intellectual search"). Tizard und Hughes (*Young Children Learning at Home and in School. 1984* London, Fontana) verwenden diesen Ausdruck in ihren Forschungen. Solange Kinder sehr jung sind, stellen sie unablässig Fragen während sie, entweder alleine oder mit ihren Eltern oder wie auch immer, einen logischen Gedankengang verfolgen. Wenn Kinder erwachsen werden, scheint sich dies noch auszuweiten. Ich habe bei meinen Studien und in Folgestudien, die ich gerade durchführe, festgestellt, dass ältere Kinder, die sich zu Hause informell bilden, etwas so lange verfolgen können, wie sie wollen. Ein Junge hat sich ein ganzes Jahr lang ausschließlich mit Chemie beschäftigt. Das ist fortgeschrittene intellektuelle Nachforschung.

Wir wissen dennoch nicht, wie Kinder durch all diese kleinen Wissensbrocken und ohne es zu merken durch informelles Lernen zum „Wissen" kommen. Es gibt vielleicht Elemente des Unterrichtens, etwa wenn ein Kind etwas fragt und wir ihm antworten. Das kann man ein Element des Unterrichtens nennen, aber es ist etwas ganz anderes, als wenn ein Elternteil sagt, „So, jetzt werde ich dir etwas beibringen."

Schlussfolgerungen
Was schließen wir aus all dem? Zwei Dinge: zum einen – soweit intellektuelle Fähigkeiten und intellektuelles Wissen einen wesentlichen Bestandteil der Kultur bilden, kann man sie sich aneignen, einfach als Teil des Aufwachsens, ohne sie von all den sozialen Dingen abzugrenzen, die die Menschen tun. Der beste Vergleich dazu ist das Sprechen lernen. Kinder lernen die Grammatik ihrer Sprache, die sehr komplex ist, ohne irgendwelchen Unterricht.

Zum zweiten – die Art des Lernens, die während der ersten Lebensjahre stattfindet, kann über das Ende der frühen Kindheit hinaus in die späteren Jahre fortgesetzt werden. Professionelle Pädagogen erkennen dies nicht. Da wird plötzlich ein Schnitt gemacht und die Kinder werden einer völlig anderen Art Pädagogik ausgesetzt. Die erste Pädagogik ist selbstgesteuert und informell. Die zweite folgt dem Schema „Ich werde dir zeigen, was du lernen musst." Die beiden sind sehr, sehr unterschiedlich.

Nachfolgende Untersuchungen
Nur als Vorgeschmack auf nachfolgende Studien - Harriet Pattison und ich schreiben momentan an einem Folgeband zu meinem ersten Buch. Die meisten Eltern, egal wie formal oder informell sie waren, sagen heute, dass sie etwas informeller hätten sein können oder sich wünschten, sie wären informeller gewesen. Das gilt allgemein, ganz egal, was die Eltern sonst sagen. Es gibt eine Reihe verschiedener Ergebnisse. Einige dieser Kinder schneiden extrem gut ab: höchste Punktzahlen bei den Eingangstests der Universitäten, etc. Andere sind

eher mittelmäßig. Was ihnen allen gemeinsam zu sein scheint, ist eine Vorstellung davon, was sie tun möchten. Jemand besteht zum Beispiel seine A-Level Tests oder etwas dem entsprechendes und wird gefragt auf welche Universität er gehen möchte. Als Antwort bekommt man vielleicht, „Ich weiß nicht. Eigentlich denke ich nicht, dass ich auf eine Universität gehen werde." Sie haben gelernt, für sich selbst Verantwortung zu übernehmen und ihre eigenen Entscheidungen zu treffen.

Home Education in France

by Jennifer Fandard

Jennifer Fandard is mother of two children who learned without school and board member of Les Enfants d'Abord, a French national home education organisation. She has a legal background and is part of a team that provides legal information and assistance for members of the organisation.

The new 1998 legislation requires annual registration with the mayor and the school academy, an investigation every two years by the mayor to determine the family's reasons for home educating, and the health of the children, as well as annual verification by the school inspector of the instruction being given. The knowledge that the children must acquire is determined by the decree of March 23, 1999. This decree lists several broad areas of knowledge, covering the subjects one would normally study in public or private schools with a State contract. Parents are not required to teach the State curriculum as such, but the objective must be to bring children to a comparable level to children in school by the end of the period of compulsory education, which is at age 16. The education given to the child must permit the development of the child's personality and must not hinder his or her socialisation.

The law also provides for heavy fines and prison sentences if the family refuses to comply with a school attendance order, after two inspections judging that the instruction is insufficient.

Most French home educators feel that their freedom has been greatly reduced by the new legislation. Nevertheless, the home education option continues to interest more and more parents and children.

Informal Learning: A French Example

by Arno and André Stern

Arno Stern was born in Kassel, in Germany, from where he emigrated to France in 1933 at the age of nine years. After spending three years in a work camp in Switzerland, he came back to France after the liberation, and entered a home for war orphans where he worked with the children. With the benefit of this first teaching experience, he founded a specific place for play in painting in Paris, called the Closlieu, where he continues his work.

He is known throughout the world, for his numerous publications, his conferences and courses, and the scientific field he created: Expression semiology.

During his fifty years of practice, he was witness to a manifestation which he called Formulation, facilitated by the particular conditions created in the Closlieu. He discovered the originality, the mechanisms and the natural origins of the Trace which he observed that people have spontaneously.

He furthered the studies in his field by living with unschooled populations in deserts, virgin forests, brush, mountainous regions, to prove the universality of Formulation.

Arno Stern opposes the Art of painting (which is the artists' field) to Play in painting, which everyone else does inherently; it is not the result of a gift and excludes no one. It stems from a natural or organic necessity possessed by human beings, and is part of their genetic program. This aptitude has been neglected and sacrificed to artistic techniques and practices which destroy spontaneity.

It was obvious for Arno Stern and Michèle, his wife, that their children would not be restricted in their natural development to any curriculum and that although these children did not go to school, the idea was not to teach them at home, but to live with them and stimulate their interests and curiosity.

Arno Stern:
Although our children's activities were not subject to a curriculum, they were varied and structured. Some were done at home; others in places which we chose for the quality they offered. So, for instance, André spent an afternoon each week in a brass workshop and learned metal-working. Later he learned photography and learned different weaving techniques with his sister. Both children learned free dancing. André studied guitar very early, with a Spanish master; Eléonore learned to play piano with Jacques Greys. Both children regularly painted in a Saturday group at the Closlieu. Eléonore learned gold leafing. When she was small, she accompanied her mother to a pillow-lace

85

workshop and became accomplished in this skill, to which she added embroidery and sewing. She learned Indian classical dance, was part of a swimming team and free-skating team with Russian trainers, and later on she learned fencing. All these activities were part of her project to become a comedian and a dancer.

These activities were practised regularly and seriously, but there was also time for all sorts of improvised play, walks, visits, reading and listening to music.

When André reached adolescence, he decided to become a lute maker. André and Eléonore, and their two cousins who were educated like them, without academic instruction, formed a group and created and presented dance shows of very high quality.

André and Eléonore learned English in an amusing way. One day a man, David, came to see me and said he was a chemist but didn't have papers to work in France. He wanted to know if I had any work in translation for him. I didn't, but I asked if he wanted to teach English to my children. He answered, "But I am not an English teacher." So I told him, "Precisely." "I have no idea how I am going to do it", he replied, "but I'll think about it." He left, but came back next day and said, "When I was young I was a comedian and I have an idea." And he came to see my children for several months and told them little stories in English. They invented short plays together. The children rolled on the ground with laughter. And this is how they learned English.

David, who in so doing, revived his former vocation as a comic, ended up finding work and could not spend any more time with our children. André wanted to continue and developed his linguistic knowledge with the Assimil method. He learned English, then German, then Spanish, then Latin. Eléonore learned Russian by the same method and then learned English with the Wall Street Institute.

How children learn
We should not think in terms of teaching like at school, using different subjects such as reading, arithmetic, geography and so on. We don't teach a little child how to speak or to walk. He or she learns to speak because he wants to communicate. Writing develops naturally, in an environment where it is routinely practised. There is no set age at which to learn how to write, nor any method necessary to acquire this capacity. Nothing is more terrible than

this idea that we must create standards and work towards a diploma, as if once the exam has been passed, all learning is finished. There is no age at which discovering new things ends.

André Stern:
Arno's son, has never been to school. Informal learning is an integral part of his life, and he gives international conferences on child-led, learner-managed learning.

I'm a musician, composer, and a guitar-maker. I work in the theatre, in the field of dance, and as an artistic director. I organise festivals. And I am an IT expert. Have I done any studies or research? My life, and Life (with a capital L) in general is learning, research. Research in order to know the world better. Research to know one's inner self better. Research for happiness or balance.

If you'd like to know about the advanced studies I've done, here is an incomplete list:
- Dance
- Brass-working
- Magic (semi-professional)
- Photography (comprehensive history, theory, chemistry, optical and mechanical aspects, taking photos, legal rights and responsibilities of photographers, development, digital processing)
- Music (history, biographies of all classic composers, theory and mechanics)
- Egyptology (studied at The College of France)
- Languages (German, Spanish, English, Latin, and of course, French)
- Stringed-instrument manufacturing (history, biographies of masters, wood and sound theory, ancient preparations and varnishes, and of course master-level instrument making)
- Electricity (theory and practice) and electronics
- Mechanics (theory and practice, cars in particular)
- Physics (quantum mechanics)
- Philosophy
- Computer science (professional level)
- Theatre (management, administration, technical aspects, lighting, directing, acting, and all aspects of the stage in general)

I don't really know how useful all these studies are, and the list is neither complete, nor (happily) is it finished.

My Home Education

I didn't just take up my parents' opinions, and if we have the same opinions it is because we came to our conclusions separately. I would like to stress this point because, about ten years ago, I took up the work of talking about home education and informal learning. My intention is not to convince you or convert you. What I have to say is simple really: I didn't go to school.

I didn't have any difficulty meeting people. The notion of meeting other children of the same age seems very school oriented to me. I met people, who were younger, older, from all walks of life, all sorts of people, people with different kinds of experiences from mine. There were people who could teach me things and there were people who I could teach. I met children. I played with children, including those who were in school when they were not in class.

We didn't have any problems with the school authorities when we were young. I think that *I* was a problem for them. How could they control someone who doesn't correspond to the established standards?

People want to know how home education and informal learning affected my childhood. I can't separate my childhood from an informal education. I can't separate my life from my informal education. My ideas are perhaps different from yours in the sense that I can't manage to distinguish between life, childhood, play, work, and learning. What do we mean when we talk about informal learning? Can learning be anything but informal? Learning is what we do every day at every instant, each of us, every living being on earth, whether human or not. We don't stop learning at the end of childhood. And anyway at what age does childhood end?

When children or adults want to learn something from me, music for instance, I adapt to each individual. I always say there is no good teacher or bad student. It is possible to have a bad teacher, but a bad student doesn't exist. Another way to say this is that if it doesn't work between the teacher and the student, it is not the fault of the teacher or the fault of the student, but the lack of chemistry between the two. So I am very attentive to this aspect of the relationship.

People worry about how anyone can grow up and eat and so forth if they don't have formal instruction. It is difficult for me to understand this because I am a very active person who earns his living. For me there is a big difference between culture and teaching – to me they are not related. Education doesn't bring us culture. Education brings a certain type of culture. I lead an active professional life and not having a scholastic education does prevent me at all from earning my living naturally.

I don't have any children yet, but when I do, their childhood will have the same freedom as mine did. This does not mean they will have the same childhood as I did. Each child has a unique childhood. My own experience is not a method nor a recipe nor a guarantee.

L'instruction à la maison en France

par Jennifer Fandard

Jennifer Fandard est mère de deux enfants qui ont appris hors école. Elle est membre du conseil d'administration de Les Enfants d'Abord, la plus grande association nationale française défendant l'instruction à la maison et fait partie de l'équipe juridique de cette association.

La nouvelle législation de 1998 exige une déclaration annuelle au maire et à l'inspection académique et une enquête tous les deux ans par le maire, afin de déterminer les raisons du choix de la famille et si l'instruction est compatible avec l'état de santé de l'enfant. Cette législation prévoit aussi une vérification annuelle de l'instruction qui est donné par les parents. Le décret du 23 mars 1999 contient les connaissances requises des enfants. Ce décret énumère plusieurs grands domaines de connaissances, couvrant des matières qu'on étudierait normalement dans des établissements publics ou privés sous contrat. Les parents ne sont pas tenus d'enseigner les programmes scolaires de l'Education nationale mais l'objet de l'enseignement doit être d'amener les enfants à un niveau comparable aux enfants scolarisés à la fin de la période d'instruction obligatoire, actuellement fixée à 16 ans. L'instruction qui est donnée à l'enfant doit lui permettre de développer sa personnalité et de s'insérer dans la vie sociale.

La loi prévoit de lourdes amendes et des peines de prison si la famille refuse d'obéir à une injonction de scolariser, suite à deux inspections jugeant que l'instruction est insuffisante.

La plupart des familles instruisant leurs enfants à la maison sont d'avis que leur liberté a été très atteinte par cette nouvelle législation. Cependant, le choix d'instruction hors école continue à intéresser de plus en plus de parents et d'enfants.

Apprentissage informel : un exemple français

par Arno et André Stern

Arno Stern est né à Kassel, en Allemagne, d'où il émigra en France en 1933 à l'âge de neuf ans. Après trois années passées dans un camp de travail en Suisse, il revient en France, à la libération, et entre dans un home pour orphelins de guerre pour y travailler avec les enfants. Fort de cette première expérience pédagogique, il fonde un espace spécifique, pour le jeu de peindre à Paris, appelé le Closlieu, où se déroule, depuis lors, son activité.

Il est connu, à travers le monde, par ses nombreuses publications, ses conférences et cours, et le domaine scientifique qu'il a créé : La Sémiologie de l'Expression.

Témoin, durant ses cinquante années de pratique, d'une manifestation que les conditions particulières du Closlieu ont pour vertu de susciter, appelée la Formulation, il découvre l'originalité, les mécanismes et les origines organiques de la Trace spontanée.

Il étend le champ de ses études en séjournant auprès de populations non-scolarisées, dans des déserts, la forêt vierge, la brousse, des contrées d'altitude, apportant la preuve de l'universalité de la Formulation.

Arno Stern oppose à l'Art de peindre (qui appartient aux artistes), le Jeu de peindre, qui est propre à tous les autres, n'est tributaire d'aucun don, n'excepte personne et découle d'une nécessité organique propre à l'humain, en prise directe avec le programme génétique. Cette aptitude a été négligée et se trouve sacrifiée à des pratiques ayant l'art pour but et qui détruisent la spontanéité.

Il était évident pour Arno Stern et Michèle, son épouse, que leurs enfants ne seraient restreints, dans leur développement naturel, par aucun programme d'enseignement et que, si ces enfants n'allaient pas à l'école, il n'était pas d'avantage question de les enseigner à la maison, mais de vivre en leur compagnie, en stimulant leurs intérêts et leurs curiosités.

Arno Stern :
Si les activités de nos enfants n'étaient pas administrées par un programme, elles étaient variées et structurées. Certaines se passaient à la maison, d'autres à l'extérieur, dans des lieux choisis pour leurs qualités : ainsi André passait une après-midi par semaine dans un atelier de dinanderie et y apprenait le travail du métal. Plus tard, il s'initiait à la photographie et, avec sa sœur, il apprenait divers modes de tissages. Les deux enfants ont été initiés à la danse, dite d'Expression. André a, très tôt, appris la guitare avec un maître espagnol, Eléonore a appris à jouer du piano avec Jacques Greys. Les deux enfants ont régulièrement peint dans le groupe du samedi dans le Closlieu. Eléonore a appris la dorure. Très petite, elle accompagnait sa maman dans un atelier de dentelle aux fuseaux et s'est perfectionnée dans ce métier, qu'elle a complété par la broderie et la couture. Elle a appris la danse classique indienne, elle a fait partie d'un club de natation et d'un autre de patinage artistique avec des maîtres russes et, plus tard, elle a fait de l'escrime. Toutes ces activités faisant partie de son projet de devenir comédienne et danseuse.

Ces activités, pratiquées régulièrement et avec beaucoup de sérieux, laissaient cependant du temps pour toutes sortes de jeux improvisés, des promenades, visites, lectures, l'écoute de la musique...

André, à l'adolescence, a décidé de devenir luthier. André et Eléonore, ainsi que leurs deux cousines – élevées, comme eux, sans instruction scolaire – ont formé un groupe et ont élaboré et présenté sur scène des spectacles de danse de très haut niveau.

André et Eléonore ont appris l'anglais de manière amusante. Un jour, un homme appelé David se présenta chez moi et m'a dit qu'il était chimiste mais sans papiers pour travailler en France. Il voulait savoir si je n'avais pas des traductions à lui faire faire. Je n'avais rien à lui proposer, mais je lui ai demandé s'il voulait bien enseigner l'anglais à mes enfants. Il m'a dit qu'il n'était pas professeur d'anglais, ce à quoi j'ai répondu : « justement ! ». « Je n'ai aucune idée de la façon de s'y prendre » me confia-t-il, « mais je vais y réfléchir ». Il est revenu le lendemain en disant : « quand j'étais jeune, j'étais acteur, j'ai une idée ». Il s'est occupé donc de mes enfants durant plusieurs mois, leur a raconté de petites histoires en anglais. Ils ont monté de courtes pièces de théâtre ensemble. Mes enfants étaient pliés de rire. C'est comme ça qu'ils ont commencé à apprendre l'anglais.

David ayant ainsi ravivé les vocations de comique de sa jeunesse, a trouvé un engagement et n'a plus eu de temps pour nos enfants. André a voulu poursuivre et a développé ses connaissances linguistiques par la méthode Assimil. Il a fait de l'anglais, puis de l'allemand, de l'espagnol et du latin. Eléonore a appris le russe par la même méthode et, plus tard, a perfectionné l'anglais au Wall Street Institut.

Comment les enfants apprennent

Il ne faut pas raisonner dans une optique d'instruction comme le fait l'école, en instaurant des matières : la lecture, le calcul, la géographie... On n'enseigne pas au petit enfant à parler, à marcher... il pratique la langue dans son désir de communiquer. L'écriture se développe aussi naturellement, dans un milieu où elle est une pratique courante. Et il n'y a pas un âge fixe pour commencer à écrire, ni une méthode pour acquérir cette capacité. Rien n'est plus terrible que le raisonnement qui crée des niveaux et vise à un diplôme, comme si, l'examen étant passé avec succès, les apprentissages étaient arrivés à leur terme. Il n'y a pas d'âge pour cesser de découvrir.

André Stern :

Le fils d'Arno n'a jamais été à l'école. L'apprentissage informel fait partie intégrante de sa vie. Il donne des conférences internationales sur l'apprentissage non dirigé et auto-géré des enfants.

Je suis musicien, compositeur et luthier. Je travaille dans le théâtre, dans le milieu de la danse, et comme directeur artistique. J'organise des festivals. Et je suis expert dans les technologies d'internet. Ai-je fait des études ou des recherches ? Ma vie, et la Vie (avec un V majuscule) toute entière, n'est qu'étude et recherche : Recherche, dans le but de mieux appréhender le monde ; recherche pour mieux se connaître ; recherche de bonheur ou d'équilibre.

Si vous voulez en savoir plus sur mes études, en voici une liste incomplète :

- danse

- dinanderie (travail du métal par martelage)
- magie (semi pro)
- photographie (histoire, théorie, chimie, optique et mécanique, prise de vues, droits et responsabilités juridiques concernant la photographie, développement, numérique)
- musique (histoire, biographies de tous les compositeurs de musique classique, théorie et mécanique)
- égyptologie (au Collège de France)
- langues (allemand, espagnol, anglais, latin et bien évidemment, français)
- manufacture d'instruments à cordes (histoire, biographies des maîtres, théorie du bois et des sons, préparation à l'ancienne, vernis et bien sur, niveau de maître dans la fabrication d'instruments)
- électricité (théorie et pratique) et électronique
- mécanique (théorie et pratique, la voiture en particulier)
- physique (mécanique quantique)
- philosophie
- technologie des ordinateurs (niveau professionnel)
- théâtre (direction, administration, technique, lumière, mise en scène, acteur et de façon plus générale, tous les aspects concernant la scène)

Je ne sais pas dans quelle mesure toutes ces études sont vraiment utiles et la liste n'est ni complète ni (heureusement) terminée.

Comment j'ai appris à la maison
Je n'ai pas simplement suivi les opinions de mes parents et si nous avons les mêmes, c'est que nous sommes arrivés aux mêmes conclusions, mais par des chemins différents. J'aimerais souligner ce point, parce qu'il y a 10 ans de cela, j'ai décidé de parler d'apprentissage informel et d'instruction à la maison. Mon intention n'est pas de vous convaincre ou de vous convertir. Ce que j'ai à dire est vraiment simple : je ne suis pas allé à l'école.

Je n'ai éprouvé aucun mal à rencontrer des gens. Ne rencontrer que des enfants de son âge c'est quelque chose de très scolaire, à mon sens. J'ai croisé des gens qui étaient plus jeunes que moi, plus âgés, qui venaient de tous horizons, qui avaient des expériences totalement différentes des miennes. Certains m'ont appris des choses et d'autres ont appris de moi. J'ai rencontré et joué avec des enfants, ceux qui allaient à l'école, je ne les voyais qu'en dehors des heures de classe.

Nous n'avons pas eu de problèmes avec les autorités scolaires quand nous étions jeunes. Je pense plutôt que c'est MOI qui étais un problème pour elles. Comment pouvaient-elles contrôler quelqu'un qui ne correspondait à aucun des étalons établis?

Les gens veulent savoir de quelle façon l'instruction en famille et l'apprentissage informel ont pu affecter mon enfance. Mais pour moi, l'un ne va pas sans l'autre. Je ne peux séparer ma vie de mon apprentissage informel. Mes idées sont peut-être différentes des vôtres, dans le sens où je ne peux faire de distinctions entre la vie, l'enfance, le jeu, le travail, et apprendre. De quoi parlons nous lorsque nous évoquons l'apprentissage informel? Est-ce que l'apprentissage peut être autre chose qu'informel? Apprendre, c'est ce que nous faisons tous les jours, à chaque moment, chacun de nous, chaque être vivant présent sur cette terre, humain ou pas. Nous ne cessons pas d'apprendre lorsque finit l'enfance. Et puis, à quel âge l'enfance s'arrête-t-elle?

Quand les enfants ou adultes veulent apprendre quelque chose de moi, la musique par exemple, je m'adapte à chaque individu. J'ai l'habitude de dire qu'il n'y a ni bon professeur ni mauvais élève. C'est possible d'avoir un mauvais professeur, mais un mauvais élève, ça n'existe pas. Une autre façon d'exprimer cela revient à dire que si ça ne marche pas entre un prof et son élève, ce n'est ni la faute de l'un, ni celle de l'autre. C'est juste un manque d'atomes crochus entre eux. Je suis donc très attentif à cet aspect de la relation.

Les gens se demandent comment on peut grandir et manger etc. sans avoir reçu une instruction formelle. C'est vraiment difficile pour moi de saisir cela, parce que je suis quelqu'un d'actif, qui gagne sa vie. Pour moi, il existe une différence énorme entre la culture et l'enseignement : ce sont deux choses absolument distinctes. L'enseignement ne nous apporte pas la culture, mais seulement un certain genre de culture. Je mène une vie professionnelle active, ne pas avoir eu d'éducation scolaire ne m'empêche aucunement de gagner naturellement ma vie.

Je n'ai pas encore d'enfants, mais lorsque je deviendrai père, leur enfance sera aussi libre que ce qu'a pu être la mienne. Cela ne veut en rien dire qu'elle sera identique. Chaque enfant à une enfance unique. Ce que j'ai vécu n'est ni une méthode, ni une recette, ni la garantie de quoi que ce soit.

Bildung zu Hause in Frankreich

von Jennifer Fandard

Jennifer Fandard ist Mutter von zwei – mittlerweile erwachsenen – Söhnen, die sich ohne Schulbesuch gebildet haben. Sie ist Vorstandsmitglied von 'Les Enfants d'Abord', eines französischen Vereines, der die Bildung zu Hause unterstützt. Sie verfügt über juristische Kenntnisse und arbeitet in einer Gruppe mit, die rechtliche Informationen sammelt und den Vereinsmitgliedern juristische Unterstützung vermittelt.

In der neuen Gesetzgebung aus dem Jahr 1998 wird von Familien, deren Kinder sich zu Hause bilden, eine jährliche Meldung beim Bürgermeister und den Schulbehörden verlangt. Alle zwei Jahre werden die Familien nach den Gründen, warum sie Bildung zu Hause als Lernweg wählen, befragt. Auch der Gesundheitszustand der Kinder wird zweijährlich überprüft. Einmal jährlich wird die Qualität der häuslichen Bildung von einem Schulinspektor geprüft. Umfang und Inhalt der Kenntnisse, welche die Kinder erlangen sollen, sind im Erlass vom 23. März 1999 festgelegt. Dieser Erlass listet eine Anzahl weitumrissener Fachbereiche auf, in denen Kinder, die öffentliche oder staatlich anerkannte Privatschulen besuchen, normalerweise unterrichtet werden. Eltern sind nicht verpflichtet, ihre Kinder nach dem staatlichen Lehrplan zu unterrichten. Das Ziel der Bildung zu Hause sollte jedoch die Erlangung eines Wissensstandes sein, der demjenigen von sechzehnjährigen Schülern mit regulärer Schullaufbahn entspricht. (Die in Frankreich bestehende Bildungspflicht gilt bis zu einem Alter von sechzehn Jahren.) Die Bildung und Erziehung, die ein Kind erhält, muss zur Entwicklung seiner Persönlichkeit beitragen und darf seine Sozialisation nicht gefährden.

Der Gesetzgeber sieht erhebliche Bußgelder und sogar Gefängnisstrafen vor, sofern Eltern der Aufforderung, ihre Kinder zur Schule zu schicken, nicht nachkommen. Eine solche Aufforderung wird fällig, sobald die Qualität des häuslichen Unterrichts vom Schulinspektor als ungenügend bewertet wurde und eine daraufhin durchgeführte zweite Überprüfung dieses Ergebnis bestätigt hat.

Die meisten französischen Familien, die sich für eine Bildung ihrer Kinder ohne Schulbesuch entscheiden, empfinden die neue Gesetzgebung als gravierenden Einschnitt in ihre Freiheitsrechte. Dennoch hält der Trend, Bildung zu Hause statt Schulbesuch zu wählen, an und interessiert immer mehr Eltern und Kinder.

Informelles Lernen:
Ein Beispiel aus Frankreich

von Arno und André Stern

Arno Stern wurde in Kassel, Deutschland geboren, von wo er 1933 im Alter von neun Jahren nach Frankreich auswanderte. Nach seiner Entlassung aus einem schweizer Arbeitslager, in dem er drei Jahre verbracht hatte, kehrte er nach Frankreich zurück und begann dort, in einem Heim für Kriegswaisen mit den Kindern zu arbeiten. Durch diese ersten pädagogischen Erfahrungen bestärkt, gründete er in Paris einen Ort eigener Art, den er 'Closlieu' (wörtlich: 'geschlossener Ort', wird im Deutschen als 'Malort' bezeichnet) nannte. Im 'Malort', den er für das sogenannte 'Malspiel' (das freie Spiel mit Farben) schuf, setzte Arno Stern seine pädagogische Arbeit fort.

Durch seine zahlreichen Publikationen, durch Konferenzen und Kurse, sowie durch den von ihm begründeten Wissenschaftszweig, die Semiologie (Theorie bzw. Lehre der Zeichen) des Ausdrucks, wurde Arno Stern welweit bekannt.

Während seiner fünfzigjährigen Praxis konnte er als Augenzeuge miterleben, wie unter den besonderen Bedingungen des 'Malorts' etwas zum Ausdruck kommen konnte, das er 'Formulation' nannte. Er hatte die Einzigartigkeit, den Mechanismus und den natürlichen Ursprung der zeichnerischen 'Spur' entdeckt, die eine universelle und spontane Ausdrucksform aller Menschen ist.

Er erweiterte seine Forschungen, indem er Bevölkerungsgruppen aufsuchte, die keine schulische Unterrichtung kennen. Er verbrachte eine Zeitlang mit den Einwohnern verschiedener Wüsten, Regenwälder, Buschgebiete und Gebirgslagen.

Arno Stern stellte der 'Kunstmalerei' (welche Ausdrucksform und Beschäftigungsfeld von Künstlern ist) das sogenannte 'Malspiel' gegenüber, welches eine allen Menschen gleichermaßen von Natur aus gegebene Ausdrucksform ist, die nicht an eine besondere Begabung gebunden ist und daher niemanden ausnimmt. Das 'Malspiel' enspringt einem natürlichen, organischen Bedürfnis des Menschen und ist ein Teil seines genetischen Programms. Diese Ausdrucksfähigkeit wird jedoch völlig vernachlässigt und wird außerdem zugunsten der Übungen, welche die Förderung des künstlerischen Ausdrucks zum Ziel haben, geopfert. Dadurch wird die Spontaneität zerstört.

Für Arno Stern und seine Frau Michèle war es klar, dass sie ihre Kinder in ihrer natürlichen Entfaltung nicht einschränken würden. Sie würden sich an keinerlei Erziehungs- oder Bildungsprogramm halten und ihre Kinder – wenn sie nicht in eine Schule gingen – auch nicht zu Hause unterrichten. Sie wollten einfach mit ihren Kindern zusammenleben und sie in ihren Interessen und ihrer Wissbegierde unterstützend begleiten.

Arno Stern:
Die Beschäftigungen unserer Kinder waren nicht durch einen Lehrplan oder irgendein Programm festgelegt, aber dennoch vielfältig und strukturiert. Es gab Beschäftigungen innerhalb und außerhalb des Hauses, an Orten, die wir aufgrund ihrer besonderen Qualitäten auswählten: so verbrachte beispielsweise André einen Nachmittag pro Woche in einer Werkstatt für Messingbearbeitung und erlernte dort den Umgang mit diesem Material. Später erlernte er die Grundlagen der Fotografie, und zusammen mit seiner Schwester erlernte er verschiedene Webtechniken. Beide Kinder begannen, Tanzunterricht zu nehmen, das heißt, sie erlernten freien Ausdruckstanz. Schon sehr früh begann André, mit einem spanischen Meister das Gitarrespiel zu lernen. Eléonore lernte Klavierspielen mit Jaques Greys. Beide Kinder malten regelmäßig in der Samstagsgruppe im 'Malort' mit. Eléonore erlernte das Vergolden. Als sie noch ganz klein war, begleitete sie ihre Mutter zu einem Spitzenklöppelkurs. Später hat sie sich in diesem Handwerk weitergebildet und erlernte zwei weitere Handarbeitstechniken, das Sticken und die Schneiderei. Sie erlernte den klassischen indischen Tanz, war Mitglied in einem Schwimmverein und in einem Eiskunstlaufverein bei russischen Meisterläufern, und später hat sie noch Fechten gelernt. All diese Beschäftigungen waren Teil ihres Vorhabens, einmal als Schauspielerin und Tänzerin tätig zu sein.

Die Kinder führten all diese Tätigkeiten regelmäßig und mit großer Ernsthaftigkeit aus. Trotzdem blieb ihnen genug Zeit zum Spielen, um Spazieren zu gehen, für Besuche, zum Lesen, um Musik zu hören und zu vielem mehr.

Als Jugendlicher entschloß sich André, Saiteninstrumentenbauer zu werden. André und Eléonore und ihre beiden Cousinen, die ebenfalls ohne Schulbesuch und ohne Unterrichtung aufwuchsen, schlossen sich zu einer Gruppe zusammen

97

und erarbeiteten Tanzvorstellungen, die sie auch aufführten, und die wirklich ein sehr hohes Niveau hatten.

Englisch lernten André und Eléonore auf sehr unterhaltsame Weise. Eines Tages stellte sich ein Mann bei mir vor, David, der mir erzählte, daß er Chemiker sei, aber keine Papiere habe, um in Frankreich zu arbeiten. Er wollte wissen, ob ich nicht Übersetzungsarbeiten für ihn hätte. Ich konnte ihm damit leider nicht weiterhelfen, aber ich fragte ihn, ob er nicht Lust hätte, meinen Kindern Englischunterricht zu geben. Er sagte mir, dass er ja kein Englischlehrer sei, worauf ich spontan antwortete: "Genau darum frage ich!" "Ich habe nicht die geringste Vorstellung davon, wie ich das anfangen sollte", gestand er mir, "aber ich werde darüber nachdenken". Am nächsten Morgen kam er zurück und sagte zu mir: "Als ich jung war, war ich Schauspieler – ich habe da eine Idee." Er hat sich dann während mehrerer Monate mit meinen Kindern beschäftigt und ihnen kleine Geschichten auf Englisch erzählt. Zusammen haben sie kurze Theaterstücke gespielt. Oft kugelten sich meine Kinder vor lauter Lachen. So haben meine Kinder angefangen, Englisch zu lernen.

David hat durch die Beschäftigung mit unseren Kindern die Berufung aus seiner Jugendzeit – als Komiker tätig zu sein – zu neuem Leben erweckt und hat ein Engagement gefunden, wodurch ihm für die Kinder keine Zeit mehr übrigblieb. André wollte weitermachen und hat seine Sprachkenntnisse mit der 'Assimil'-Methode vertieft. Er hat erst Englisch gelernt, dann Deutsch, Spanisch und Latein. Eléonore hat mit der selben Methode Russisch gelernt und hat später ihr Englisch am 'Wall Street Insitute' perfektioniert.

Wie Kinder lernen

Es ist unsinnig, von Überlegungen auszugehen, die das Augenmerk auf Unterricht richten, wie er in der Schule gegeben wird, also auf die Unterweisung in einzelnen Fächern wie Lesen, Rechnen, Erdkunde usw. Man bringt ja auch keinem Kind das Sprechen und das Laufen bei, man unterrichtet das Kind nicht hierin – das Kind benützt – und übt dabei automatisch – die Sprache, weil es sich mit den Anderen verständigen möchte. Auch das Schreiben entwickelt sich auf die gleiche, natürliche Weise, wenn man in einer Umgebung lebt, wo Schreiben eine allgemein gebräuchliche Fertigkeit ist. Und es gibt kein Alter, das am besten dazu geeignet wäre, um mit dem Schreibenlernen zu beginnen, genausowenig wie eine bestimmte Methode nötig ist, um diese Fähigkeit zu erlangen. Es gibt nichts Schrecklicheres als die gängige Argumentation, die dazu beiträgt, dass Standards festgelegt werden und alles Lernen auf das Erreichen eines Abschlusszeugnisses ausgerichtet wird: Als ob nach einem erfoglreichen Schulabschluss das Lernen sein Ziel und damit ein Ende erreicht hätte. Es gibt kein Alter, um mit dem Entdecken, dem Erlernen von neuen Dingen aufzuhören.

André Stern:

Arnos Sohn war nie in der Schule. Informelles Lernen ist ein integraler Bestandteil seines Lebens. Er veranstaltet internationale Konferenzen, die das nichtdirektive und selbstbestimmte kindliche Lernen zum Thema haben.

Ich bin Musiker, Komponist und Gitarrenbauer. Ich arbeite im Theater, in der Sparte Tanz, und als künstlerischer Leiter. Ich organisiere Festivals. Und ich bin IT-Experte (Fachmann für Internet-Technologien). Habe ich irgendwelche Studien oder Forschungen unternommen? Mein ganzes Leben – und das Leben an sich – ist nichts anderes als Studium und Forschung: Forschung, die zum Ziel hat, die Welt besser zu verstehen; Forschung um sich selbst besser kennenzulernen; Streben nach Glück oder Ausgeglichenheit.

Wenn Sie mehr über meine Studien wissen möchten, so gebe ich Ihnen hier einmal eine unvollständige Liste:

- Tanz
- Messingtreibarbeiten (Metallbearbeitung durch Hämmern)
- Zauberei (halb-professionell)
- Fotografie (Geschichte, Theorie, Chemie, Optik und Mechanik, fotografische Aufnahmen, Rechte und rechtliche Verantwortlichkeiten in der Fotografie, Entwicklung, Digitalfotografie)
- Musik (Geschichte, Biographien aller Komponisten klassischer Musik, Theorie und Mechanik)
- Ägyptologie (am 'Collège de France')
- Sprachen (Deutsch, Spanisch, Englisch, Latein und selbstverständlich Französisch)
- Saiteninstrumentenbau (Geschichte, Meisterbiographien, Holztheorie und Klangtheorie, Herstellung in altertümlichem Stil, Lackierung und natürlich Instrumentenbau auf Meisterniveau)
- Elektrik (Theorie und Praxis) und Elektronik
- Mechanik (Theorie und Praxis, insbesondere Autos)
- Physik (Quantenmechanik)
- Philosophie
- Computer-Technik (professionelles Niveau)

- Theater (Leitung, Verwaltung, Technik, Beleuchtung, Regieführung, Schauspieler, und ganz allgemein: alle Aspekte rund um die Bühne)

Ich weiß nicht, in welcher Hinsicht all diese Studien wirklich nützlich sind, und diese Liste ist weder vollständig noch (glücklicherweise) endgültig.

We ich zu Hause gelernt habe

Ich habe mich nicht einfach den Meinungen meiner Eltern angeschlossen, und wenn wir heutzutage die gleichen Meinungen vertreten dann deshalb, weil wir zu den gleichen Schlussfolgerungen gekommen sind, allerdings auf verschiedenen (eigenen) Wegen. Weil ich mich vor zehn Jahren dazu entschlossen habe, über informelles Lernen und Bildung zu Hause zu sprechen, möchte ich diesen Punkt besonders betonen. Ich will Sie nicht überzeugen oder in irgendeiner Weise bekehren. Was ich zu sagen habe, ist wirklich ganz einfach – ich bin nicht in die Schule gegangen.

Es fiel mir überhaupt nicht schwer, andere Menschen zu treffen. Meiner Meinung nach hat es etwas sehr 'Schulisches' an sich, wenn man sich nur mit Gleichaltrigen trifft. Ich begegnete Menschen, die jünger oder älter waren als ich, die aus allen gesellschaftlichen Kreisen kamen, die völlig andere Erfahrungen gemacht hatten als ich selbst. Manche haben mir etwas beigebracht, andere haben von mir gelernt. Ich habe mich mit Kindern getroffen und mit ihnen gespielt. Diejenigen, die in die Schule gingen, traf ich eben nur außerhalb der Unterrichtszeiten.

Wir hatten keine Probleme mit den Schulbehörden, als wir jung waren. Ich denke, dass eher ICH ein Problem für sie darstellte. Wie konnten sie jemanden kontrollieren, der in keine der üblichen 'Schubladen' passte?

Die Leute wollen wissen, inwieweit familiäre häusliche Bildung und informelles Lernen meine Kindheit beeinflusst haben. Für mich gehört beides zusammen. Ich kann mein Leben nicht von meiner Art, beiläufig und in lebendigen Zusammenhängen zu lernen, trennen. Darin, daß ich keinen Unterschied zwischen Leben, Kindheit, Arbeit und Lernen machen kann, unterscheiden sich meine Vorstellungen vielleicht von den Ihren. Wovon sprechen wir eigentlich, wenn wir den Ausdruck 'informelles Lernen' verwenden? Kann Lernen anders als auf beiläufige Art und in lebendigen

Zusammenhängen ablaufen? Lernen ist das, was wir täglich machen, in jedem Moment unseres Lebens, jeder unter uns, jedes lebendige Wesen auf dieser Erde, ob menschlich oder nicht. Wir hören nicht mit dem Ende der Kindheit auf zu lernen. Und außerdem – mit welchem Alter endet 'Kindheit' eigentlich?

Wenn Kinder oder Erwachsene etwas von mir lernen wollen – zum Beispiel Musik – stelle ich mich auf jeden Einzelnen ein. Ich pflege zu sagen, dass es weder gute Lehrer noch schlechte Schüler gibt. Es kann vorkommen, dass man einen schlechten Lehrer hat – aber ein schlechter Schüler, das gibt es nicht. Um es mit anderen Worten auszudrücken: Wenn es zwischen einem Lehrer und seinem Schüler nicht gut läuft, ist das weder der Fehler des einen noch des anderen, sondern liegt ganz einfach daran, daß die Chemie zwischen beiden nicht stimmt. Ich achte daher besonders sorgfältig auf diesen Aspekt der Beziehung.

Die Leute wundern sich, wie man aufwachsen und essen und all das kann, wenn man keinen angeleiteten, strukturierten Unterricht erhalten hat. Ich kann diese Zweifel nur schwerlich begreifen, weil ich jemand bin, der aktiv ist und seinen Lebensunterhalt verdient. Für mich besteht ein Riesen-Unterschied zwischen 'Bildung' und 'Unterricht' – das sind zwei völlig unterschiedliche Dinge. 'Unterrichtung' schafft nicht 'Bildung', durch 'Unterrichtung' wird nur eine bestimmte Art von 'Bildung' erreicht. Ich führe ein aktives Berufsleben, und der Umstand, dass ich keine schulische Ausbildung gehabt habe, hindert mich nicht im Geringsten daran, ganz selbstverständlich meinen Lebensunterhalt zu verdienen.

Ich habe noch keine Kinder, aber wenn ich Vater werden sollte, wäre ihre Kindheit genauso frei wie es meine eigene sein konnte. Was überhaupt nicht heißt, dass ihre und meine Kindheit identisch wären. Jedes Kind hat eine Kindheit, die einzigartig ist. Was ich erlebt habe, ist weder eine Methode, noch ein Rezept, noch eine Garantie – für was auch immer.

Home Education in Germany

by Stefanie Mohsennia

Stefanie Mohsennia is a librarian, home educating mother, author of "Schulfrei : Lernen ohne Grenzen" (a comprehensive introduction to home education) and webmaster of the German web site www.unschooling.de which features home education articles, laws, books, links, gatherings and events.

In Germany home education is still illegal more than 65 years after Hitler declared school attendance compulsory in 1939. Home education is nevertheless alive in Germany and there is a growing home education community in our country with estimates ranging between 500 and 3000 children.

There are two main groups of home educators. A considerable percentage of families in Germany have chosen to educate their children at home for religious reasons. These families can benefit from substantial support through Schulunterricht zu Hause e.V. (Schuzh), a national organisation that is affiliated with the American Home School Legal Defense Association which offers legal counselling in issues related to homeschooling. Often, Christian families adopt a 'school-at-home' home educating style and enrol their children in correspondence schools. A number of families is registered with the Deutsche Fernschule, the only officially recognized German correspondence school. This school is not supposed to serve families in Germany though, but missionary or diplomat families living abroad. Others are enrolled at the Philadelphia-Schule, a Christian correspondence school presently serving 300 pupils from all over the country that has been operating for 25 years without the approval of German school authorities.

Autonomous educators form another large group. These families are determined to trust their children's ability to learn whatever they need. They favour informal, child-led, interest-based learning. Autonomous learning is still a very young movement in Germany though. People are just starting to seek out like-minded families as more and more parents turn towards natural learning. Regular get-togethers on a local basis are practically non-existent as home educators are still scarce and scattered all over the country. A group of home educating parents in the south of Germany have lately started to organize field trips. The Association for Natural Learning (Bundesverband Natürliches Lernen) organizes national gatherings and a family camp in summer which an average of 20 to 40 families attend. A mailing list and a paper newsletter, issued by the Initiative für selbstbestimmtes Lernen (Initiative for autonomous learning), serve as the principal means of communication between autonomous educators. Since 2004, Clonlara School from Michigan, USA has extended their services to assist German families.

Slowly but surely, the idea of children learning at home is starting to spread in Germany. In the past year, home educators have been in the media more often. Part of the coverage has been neutral, some even positive.

On the occasion of the Kassel home education experts' meeting in January 2006, action has been taken to create a closer network between home educating families in Germany and to coordinate public relations and efforts to get the movement more organized.

© Stefanie Mohsennia, 2006

Home Education and Learner-Managed Learning: An example from Germany

by Elisabeth Kuhnle

Elisabeth Kuhnle is a home educating mother of an eleven year old boy and an eight year old girl. She lives in Karlsruhe, Germany, and has been home educating for three years. She spoke to us in English.

Home Education in Germany

In Germany, we have a particular situation for two reasons. The first is that home education is illegal. The second is that most families who choose to home education do so for religious reasons and these families are mostly practising school-at-home. Informal learning is a very new phenomenon here. There are only a few families who are home educating using informal learning. These families, unfortunately, are spread across Germany, so that there is little opportunity for any connection between them. The contact that exists is on a family-to-family basis. There is no countrywide network. The current situation in Germany influences how I actually live with my children.

The most important thing we should struggle for in Germany is that people come to know that home education is possible because most people do not know that it exists anywhere. Even teachers and school administrators don't know about it.

I think that there are a lot of families with younger children not of school age, who believe in informal learning and who are considering 'family' in a positive manner (at least more positive than people of my age usually do) and who are interested in home education for those reasons. For the moment, they don't put their children into kindergarten. This is already a first step for a lot of families to say 'no' to the system.

Networking
As I have said, informal learners here have no real network whereas, the religious home educating families and their networks stretch back almost twenty years. Informal learners started thinking about organising only two or three years ago. Networks are only now beginning to grow and it is difficult.

With two families living near Heidelberg and in Mannheim which both are not far from us, we meet more or less regularily. One of these families began their home education with the school-at-home model. Then they saw that school-at-home was not really good for their children, and they began to give the children more freedom. So you can see that parents are learning from the reactions of their children. And more, if people, that is, families with different views meet, they can exchange their views, exchange what they are learning about their life, and what they observe with their children. These exchanges help parents to be able to change the ways they treat their children. These exchanges are very interesting to me. So now, I like to be with families who are perhaps from different ideologies, but who live not too far away.

Another thing I did was to join a French home education association, 'Les Enfants D'Abord'. Once a month, we go to Strasbourg to a meeting at a member's home. This family's children are "unschoolers". It was very important for me to meet French home educators, because a lot of the French families have children who have lived without going to school all of their lives or for a long time. The families' experiences with education in this association range from children who were at school and left school, children who were at home and went back to school, children who have never been to school, "unschoolers", school-at-homers, everything. This is very interesting and very important.

Learning About Informal Learning

At this time, my children and I like very much to meet with other families with children who are not at school. We like to meet families who have this experience and who do interesting and nice things together. Two weeks ago, we went north of Frankfurt on a field trip to visit a Roman fort in Germany. There was the possibility of joining a guided tour through the different buildings of the fort especially for children. Besides, one of the mothers had prepared small workshops – for example making leather sandals - which the children could join if they felt like doing so. And we were walking around this fort and a little bit around this old site. I, as a grown up person, became aware how it is if you go to a place and you can **feel** things. You are not learning them from a book or from a teacher. You are there where history was played out, and you feel things. And even if you forget about this field trip, I think this feeling will be inside you forever where the words may be lost.

With small things like this I learn about learning by and for myself. I learn more and more about informal learning and how it works. For example, my son, who is eleven years old, told me about one and a half years ago, "I want to learn English, I want to learn French." But he was not really interested in following a course. Sometimes he said he wanted to follow a course and sometimes he didn't want to. Only a few days ago, he was in another room and he was speaking an English sentence. This sentence was not 'correct', but I asked him where he learned the words? He picked them up, maybe in songs or on the computer, I don't know, but it was very interesting. And this is what I felt myself on the field trip. If you are inside the things, and if learning is inside your life, then you are learning with what I will call "feeling", though I don't know what is the correct term.

My daughter is handicapped. If I hadn't had a handicapped daughter, I think my son would still go to school. But with my daughter I saw there was no need to put anything inside a child. The child comes and everything that is inside the child will come out in its own time. More precisely: I have the impression that children know and show themselves when they are ready to evolve new skills and to grasp new knowledge. My daughter showed me, in a sense, how learning can be.

Another thing is, the more I think about learning and school and all, the more I have the impression there is no need to think and discuss about learning. Learning is not where we must concentrate, because learning is an integral part of life. We should concentrate on other things. However, we have to discuss learning because of authorities that think that we have to send children to school. This is the only reason why we have to discuss learning and how it works, because the authorities think children only learn when they are taught inside a school.

And so, on the whole, I think this is not a German phenomenon, but a phenomenon in all industrial nations. Scientists are working on how the brain works, how a brain learns. To do so, they are invading the brain; they are invading people. They are dividing everything. If scientists and society were only behaving this way to get knowledge about how we learn, I would agree with what they are doing. However, their research is aimed at programmes to find out how people can function better. I don't agree with this. Nobody has to think about another person, about how this person can function better. I'm not sure function is the correct term, but no one has to think how another person can be better, because everything is already inside the person. So I think that no one has the right to make programmes for others. No one has the right to think for others. You can only accompany others in their life learning.

At this time, this is my interest here in Germany: to find other people to exchange these thoughts with and to work together with them. We have a discussion list on the internet (an internet discussion list) and we are thinking of creating a newspaper.

Our Family

I can think about theoretical or ideological things, but the children are just at home. Of course they also have a lot of contact outside the home. My son goes, for example, to music school. He wanted very much to learn to play the harp and we thought about how to go about it and he decided to go to music school. He also goes to crafts and handcrafts and meets friends. He is very independent, not only in his learning, but also travelling by himself.

I take my daughter to therapists. I don't think it is really necessary, but we have very good people who give these therapies and my daughter likes them, and therefore I go there. Some weeks ago, we started going one afternoon a week to a school; it is a school for mentally handicapped children. My daughter joins a group of six other children of her age, between seven and eight, only in the afternoon for one hour and a half.

My son was in school for one and a half years, so he knows what school is. He went to school because I didn't know at the time that it was possible to keep one's children at home. So, now my daughter goes to school a little and she likes to meet other children, which with her handicap is very difficult for her. Another reason for putting her in school is that the education authority and the youth welfare service like it when you co-operate a bit with them. They like it, if you see what they have to offer. I thought, if my daughter likes it, then the experience would be good for her as it is only for ninety minutes a week.

At this school they go out and play in the afternoon or do some sports; it's not really school, but it is within the school programme. It is clear to me that my daughter won't go to school for the whole week, or even for a whole day, and she will continue to go only if she likes it. I can also imagine that she won't go. For her, it depends on her need for contact with other children, as at home she is very alone.

This is how we live as a family and how the children learn is not important. Sometimes I ask myself whether my son will miss anything by not going to school. When I think very realistically, I realise he is not missing anything. Sometimes we talk about this and I ask him if he would like to try this or that (for example to follow a programme). Mostly he tells me "No, I'll do my own thing and I'll do it on my own". He is not interested in joining a school programme, or learning with a computer or distance-learning programme.

Last summer would have been his fourth year in school. The fourth term in Germany is the end of primary school. The school authorities asked if they could test him and I told them he does not follow a curriculum. I do not instruct him in anything. When the lady to whom I spoke understood our way, she decided to do an oral test. He had very, very good results. They were astonished. They offered him a place in a higher-level school (in Germany it is called the 'Gymnasium', the highest level school). They offered to let him go to 'Gymnasium' without special testing, normally you would have to pass an entrance examination. We thought about it and immediately I had the feeling it was not a good idea, because my son is still too young. It would destroy everything, if he went there every day. So I told the person concerned it

107

wouldn't be possible.

Then she offered to let him join a few classes in subjects he would like to learn like Art, English, or German or classes he could choose. So we thought about it and another summer is coming and he is still at home and didn't go to the school even for only a few classes. I think it was a good decision not to go there. I have the impression that if he began to sit in a classroom of thirty pupils and to learn in forty-five minute classes, and to hear everything from the teacher, and to see everything on a blackboard, then he will lose something.

Dissatisfaction with Schools

Germans are taking their children out of school because they are dissatisfied with schools, as in other European countries. About a month ago, I met a woman who took her son out of school, but the son is now seventeen so this was a long time ago. She took him out of school because he had had so many problems. Though she had tried so hard to find a way to keep him in school, it just was not possible. She was forced to take her son out of school as this was the only way to stop his suffering and then they travelled through Europe. She went out of the country to avoid legal and political problems. She told me she had to teach her son at home or he would not have learned anything. She was teaching him in a school-at-home style, but not for religious reasons.

I think there must be more families like this, but normally you don't know about these families because they hide. Also this woman I was speaking of told me she would not like to give anyone her telephone number or to be known until next year when her son will be eighteen. She does not want any trouble.

I know only a few families from the home-school group whose children never went to school (even not in the beginning). Most families have taken their children out of school because of bad experiences and because they met other home educated children. One family's children were in the fourth and second years and the parents took them out of school. Some informal learners took their children out of school because the children themselves simply refused to go.

My son was eight years old when he left school. And although he told me he didn't like going to school and that he wanted to stop, if I had told him, "No. You have to go!" he would have gone, I am sure. It was mainly my decision. I wanted to stop the situation, because he became a bit ill in school. We were all going crazy at home because of school.

I think a lot of children become ill in school and most parents force them to go anyway. If they are not able to go, the parents give them medicine. Only a few of them will challenge school itself and permit their children to stay at home, at least for a while. Only yesterday, on our internet discussion list, a woman wrote that they had a child, for whom they were caring. He had stopped going to school, because he suffered so much in school. He suffered so much that the school authorities agreed to allow him to stop going to school. The family was not punished or anything. Sometimes you hear of cases like this, but mostly families who take their children out of school will face difficulties and therefore they sometimes hide.

What If My Child Wants to Go to School?
As an informal home educator, what would I do if my son wanted to go to school, you ask? I would tell him this: "If you are able to get up in the morning on your own, if you are able to hear the alarm clock, and if you are able to prepare everything by yourself, you can go. But as for me, I am not going to try to make you get up." I have to shout at least ten times for my son to get up, you see, as he is a sound sleeper. If he could do this on his own it would be okay. I think it is possible now that he is eleven that he will want to go to school at some point, because he is a person who is academically oriented. And he likes to be normal. So it is possible he will go to school.

But also I think when he does go to school, after having been able to do everything on his own at home, after two weeks he will see that school is all a big mess. He will see that he won't really get anything good out of it. I think he will recognise very quickly that he won't profit from school learning because he is already used to making his own plans and living by his own rhythm. I think it is very important to find your own rhythm. The problem is that school divides subjects into small classes: forty-five minutes Maths, forty-five minutes German – this is nonsense. It is only possible to submit to this nonsense if you want to do something specific, for example a particular job.

The Future
If my son wants to have a career in something specific, for example, if he wants to work as an artist or learn about physics, we should find a place where he can work with someone on those subjects. Only in this way, I think, can he adapt to another rhythm, because he will see that he will benefit from this change. There is a big difference between this and school where everything is artificial. You

can learn to live by a 'foreign' rhythm, if you go to someone who lives his or her life doing what he or she wants to do. Even if what someone does is hard work, but work that he or she chose to do (or perhaps even life showed him or her to do it) and which is making **sense** to be done, then you can learn to live by a different rhythm.

L'instruction à la maison en Allemagne

par Stefanie Mohsennia
Stefanie Mohsennia est bibliothécaire, mère instruisant ses enfants à la maison, auteur de "Schulfrei : Lernen ohne Grenzen" ("Pas d'école : apprendre sans frontière"), (une introduction complète à l'instruction à la maison) et gérante du site internet allemand : www.unschooling.de, présentant des articles sur l'instruction à la maison, des lois, des livres, des liens, des rencontres et événements.

En Allemagne l'école à la maison est toujours illégale, plus de 65 ans après qu'Hitler a déclaré l'école obligatoire en 1939. Cependant l'instruction à la maison en Allemagne est bien vivante, et il y a une communauté croissante de personnes la pratiquant dans notre pays, dont on estime le nombre entre 500 et 3000 enfants.

Il y a deux groupes principaux de familles qui pratiquent l'instruction à domicile. Un pourcentage considérable de familles en Allemagne a choisi d'éduquer leurs enfants à la maison pour des raisons religieuses. Ces familles peuvent bénéficier d'un soutien important de Schulunterricht zu Hause e.V. (Schuzh) ('Enseignement scolaire à la maison'), une organisation nationale affiliée à l'association américaine de défense de l'école à la maison (Home School Legal Defense Association) qui offre une assistance légale aux problèmes relatifs à l'instruction à domicile. Souvent, les familles chrétiennes adoptent un style d'instruction comparable à celui de l'école et inscrivent leurs enfants dans des écoles par correspondance. Un certain nombre de familles est déclaré auprès de la Deutsche Fernschule ('Ecole par correspondance allemande'), la seule école par correspondance allemande reconnue officiellement. Pourtant cette école n'est pas censée être utilisée par les familles en Allemagne, mais par les familles missionnaires ou familles de diplomates vivant à l'étranger. D'autres enfants sont inscrits à la Philadelphia-Schule, une école chrétienne par correspondance comptant actuellement 300 élèves issus de tout le pays et qui a fonctionné pendant 25 ans sans l'agrément des autorités scolaires allemandes.

Les personnes qui instruisent leurs enfants de manière informelle forment l'autre groupe. Ces familles sont déterminées à faire confiance à la capacité de leurs enfants à apprendre ce qui leur est nécessaire. Elles favorisent l'informel, le chemin personnel de l'enfant, l'apprentissage basé sur l'intérêt. L'apprentissage informel est encore un très jeune mouvement en Allemagne. Les gens commencent depuis peu à établir un réseau de contacts à mesure que de plus en plus de parents se tournent vers l'apprentissage naturel. Des rencontres locales régulières sont pratiquement inexistantes car les familles instruisant à la maison sont encore rares et éparpillées à travers le pays. Un groupe de parents pratiquant l'instruction en famille dans le sud de l'Allemagne, dont certains n'ont pas adopté l'instruction informelle, a dernièrement organisé des sorties éducatives. L'Association pour l'apprentissage naturel (Bundesverband Natürliches Lernen) organise des rencontres nationales et un camp d'été qui compte en moyenne 20 à 40 familles participantes. Une liste de discussion internet et un journal, émis par l'Initiative pour l'apprentissage autonome (Initiative für selbstbestimmtes Lernen), servent de principaux moyens de communication entre les personnes instruisant de manière informelle. Depuis 2004, l'école Clonlara (Clonlara School) du Michigan aux Etats-Unis, a étendu ses services à l'Allemagne pour aider les familles allemandes.

Doucement, mais sûrement, l'idée de l'instruction en famille est en train de se propager à travers l'Allemagne. Depuis quelques mois, les médias s'intéressent plus fréquemment aux familles instruisant leurs enfants à la maison. Une partie de cette couverture médiatique a été neutre, mais certains articles ont été positifs.

A l'occasion de la réunion des experts en matière d'instruction à la maison qui a eu lieu à Kassel en janvier 2006, il a été décidé de créer un réseau plus rapproché entre les familles instruisant leurs enfants à la maison en Allemagne et de coordonner les relations publiques et les efforts pour que le mouvement soit plus organisé.

© Stefanie Mohsennia, 2006

L'instruction en famille et l'apprentissage auto-géré : Un exemple venant d'Allemagne

par Elisabeth Kuhnle

Elisabeth Kuhnle instruit à la maison ses deux enfants de onze et huit ans. Elle habite à Karlsruhe en Allemagne et fait l'instruction en famille depuis trois ans. Elle nous a parlé en anglais.

L'instruction en famille en Allemagne

En Allemagne nous avons une situation particulière pour deux raisons. La première est que l'instruction en famille est illégale. La deuxième est que la majorité des familles qui choisissent l'instruction en famille le font pour des raisons religieuses et ces familles font 'l'école-à-la-maison'. L'apprentissage informel est un phénomène tout à fait nouveau ici. Peu de familles dont les enfants ne vont pas à l'école les laissent apprendre de manière informelle. Ces familles sont malheureusement éparpillées à travers l'Allemagne ce qui fait qu'il y a peu d'opportunités de connexion entre elles. Les contacts qui existent se font de famille à famille. Il n'y a pas de réseau national. La situation actuelle en Allemagne influence la façon dont je vis avec mes enfants.

Le plus important pour l'Allemagne est que les gens apprennent que l'instruction hors école est possible parce que la plupart des gens ne savent pas que ça existe ici ou ailleurs. Même les enseignants et les administrateurs d'école ne connaissent pas ce mode d'instruction.

Je crois qu'il y a beaucoup de familles avec des enfants en dessous de l'âge scolaire qui croient à l'apprentissage informel et qui voient 'la famille' d'une manière positive (plus positive que les gens de mon âge, au moins), et qui, pour cela, s'intéressent à l'instruction en famille. Pour le moment ils ne mettent pas leurs enfants en maternelle. C'est déjà un premier pas pour beaucoup de familles pour dire 'non' au système.

Former un réseau

Comme je l'ai dit, les familles favorisant l'apprentissage informel ici n'ont pas de réseau réel. Alors qu'il existe depuis presque vingt ans, des familles religieuses instruisant elles-mêmes leurs enfants et leurs regroupements, les familles suivant un apprentissage informel ont seulement commencé à penser à s'organiser il y a deux ou trois ans. La formation d'un réseau commence seulement maintenant à grandir et c'est difficile.

Assez régulièrement, nous nous rencontrons avec deux familles vivant près de Heidelberg et à Mannheim, toutes les deux non loin de chez nous. Une de ces familles a commencé l'instruction hors école avec la méthode 'école-à-la-maison'. Puis ils ont vu que 'l'école-à-la-maison' n'était pas vraiment bonne pour leurs enfants et ils ont commencé à leur donner plus de liberté. Donc on voit que les parents apprennent à partir des réactions de leurs enfants. De plus, si les familles avec des points de vue différents se rencontrent, elles peuvent échanger leurs idées, échanger ce qu'elles apprennent sur leur vie, et ce qu'elles observent chez leurs enfants. Ces échanges aident les parents à pouvoir changer leur façon de traiter leurs enfants. Je les trouve très intéressants, et maintenant, j'aime bien rencontrer des familles qui ont peut-être d'autres idéologies, mais qui ne vivent pas trop loin.

Je fais aussi partie d'une association française défendant la liberté d'instruction, 'Les Enfants D'Abord'. Une fois par mois, nous allons à Strasbourg pour une rencontre chez un des membres. Les enfants de cette famille sont des 'unschoolers'. Il était très important pour moi de rencontrer des familles françaises instruisant leurs enfants à domicile parce que beaucoup de familles françaises ont des enfants qui ont vécu toute leur vie ou bien longtemps sans aller à l'école. Cette association regroupe des familles ayant des expériences avec des enfants qui ont été à l'école, mais qui l'ont quitté, des enfants qui étaient à la maison et sont retournés à l'école, des enfants qui ne sont jamais allés à l'école, des 'unschoolers', des 'écoliers-à-la-maison', donc toutes sortes d'expériences. Ceci est très intéressant et très important.

Découvrir l'apprentissage informel
En ce moment, mes enfants et moi aimons beaucoup rencontrer d'autres familles dont les enfants ne vont pas à l'école. Nous aimons rencontrer des familles qui ont cette expérience et qui font des choses intéressantes et agréables ensemble. Il y a deux semaines, nous avons fait un voyage au nord de Frankfort pour visiter un fort romain en Allemagne. On avait la possibilité de participer à une visite guidée adaptée aux enfants, à travers divers bâtiments du fort. En plus, une des mères avait préparé des petits ateliers – par exemple la fabrication de sandales en cuir simples – qu'on pouvait joindre volontairement. Nous nous promenions autour de ce fort et un peu autour de ce vieux site et

moi, en tant qu'adulte, je me suis rendue compte comment c'est d'être à un endroit où l'on peut **ressentir** des choses. On n'est pas en train d'être enseigné par un livre ou un instituteur. On est là où l'histoire s'est déroulée et on ressent quelque chose. Et même si on oublie ce voyage, je crois qu'on garde ce sentiment en soi pour toujours alors que les mots peuvent être perdus.

Avec de petites expériences comme celle-là j'apprends ce qu'est apprendre par et pour moi-même. J'apprends de plus en plus sur l'apprentissage informel et comment ça marche. Par exemple, mon fils de onze ans m'a dit, il y a environ un an: "Je veux apprendre l'anglais et je veux apprendre le français." Mais suivre un cours ne l'intéressait pas vraiment. Parfois il disait qu'il voulait suivre un cours et parfois il disait qu'il ne le voulait pas. Il y a quelques jours, il était dans une autre pièce et il a prononcé une phrase en anglais. Cette phrase n'était pas 'correcte', mais je lui ai demandé où il avait appris les mots. Il les a trouvés, peut-être dans une chanson ou sur l'ordinateur, je ne sais pas, mais c'était très intéressant. C'est cela que j'ai ressenti pendant le voyage au fort. Si on expérimente directement les choses et si apprendre est dans sa vie, alors on apprend avec ce que j'appelle le 'sentiment', bien que je ne connaisse pas le terme correct.

Ma fille est handicapée. Si je n'avais pas eu une fille handicapée, je pense que mon fils serait toujours à l'école. Mais avec ma fille j'ai vu que ce n'était pas la peine d'inculquer quoi que ce soit à un enfant. L'enfant arrive et tout ce qui est dans l'enfant en sortira le moment venu. Plus précisément: il me semble que les enfants savent et montrent eux-mêmes quand ils sont prêts à développer de nouvelles capacités et à assimiler de nouvelles connaissances. Ma fille m'a montrée, en quelque sorte, comment apprendre pouvait être.

Plus je réfléchis sur l'apprentissage et sur l'école, plus j'ai l'impression qu'il n'y a pas besoin de réfléchir à la manière d'apprendre. Ce n'est pas sur l'apprentissage que nous devons nous concentrer, parce qu'apprendre fait partie intégrale de la vie. On devrait pouvoir se concentrer sur d'autres choses. Toutefois nous sommes obligés de discuter de l'apprentissage à cause du gouvernement qui pense que nous devons envoyer les enfants à l'école. La seule raison pour laquelle nous sommes obligés de discuter de l'apprentissage et comment ça marche est que le gouvernement nous y oblige, supposant que les enfants n'apprennent que par des professeurs et dans des bâtiments scolaires.

Et je ne pense pas que ce soit un phénomène allemand, mais un phénomène dans toutes les nations industrielles. Les scientifiques étudient le fonctionnement du cerveau et comment le cerveau apprend. Pour ce faire, ils envahissent le cerveau, ils envahissent les gens. Ils divisent tout. Si les scientifiques et la société faisaient ces recherches pour savoir comment nous apprenons, je serais d'accord avec ce qu'ils font. Toutefois, leurs recherches ont pour but de créer des programmes pour découvrir comment les gens peuvent mieux fonctionner. Je ne suis pas d'accord avec ça. Personne n'a à réfléchir à propos d'une autre personne, à comment cette autre personne pourrait mieux fonctionner. Je ne suis pas sûre que fonctionner soit le mot juste, mais personne n'a à penser à comment une autre personne pourrait être mieux, parce que tout est déjà dans la personne. Donc je pense que personne n'a le droit de faire des programmes pour autrui. Personne n'a le droit de penser pour autrui. On ne peut qu'accompagner les autres dans leur apprentissage de la vie.

Pour le moment, ce qui m'intéresse ici en Allemagne : trouver d'autres personnes pour échanger ces idées et travailler avec eux. Nous avons une liste de discussion internet (circulaire par email) et pensons créer un journal.

Notre famille
Je peux penser à des théories ou à des idéologies, mais les enfants sont tout simplement à la maison. Bien entendu, ils ont aussi beaucoup de contacts en dehors de la maison. Mon fils, par exemple, va à l'école de musique. Il s'enthousiasmait pour apprendre à jouer de la harpe et nous avons réfléchi à comment il pouvait s'y prendre. Il a décidé d'aller à l'école de musique. Il fait aussi des ateliers d'arts plastiques ou il retrouve des amis. Il est très indépendant, non seulement dans ses études mais il voyage aussi tout seul.

J'emmène ma fille voir des thérapeutes. Je ne pense pas que ce soit vraiment nécessaire mais les thérapeutes sont sympas et ma fille les aime bien, et donc nous y allons. Il y a quelques semaines nous avons commencé à aller un après-midi par semaine à une école; c'est une école pour les enfants handicapés mentaux. Ma fille rejoint un groupe de six enfants de son âge, entre sept et huit ans, seulement l'après-midi pour une heure et demi.

Mon fils a été à l'école pendant un an et demi, alors il sait ce que c'est que l'école. Il est allé à l'école parce qu'à l'époque je ne savais pas qu'il était possible de garder ses enfants à la maison. Maintenant ma fille va à l'école un peu et elle aime rencontrer d'autres enfants, ce qui est difficile à cause de son handicap. Une autre raison de la mettre à l'école est que les autorités scolaires et les services des jeunes aiment qu'on coopère un peu avec eux. Ils aiment bien que l'on voie ce qu'ils ont à offrir. J'ai pensé que si ma fille aimait bien y aller, l'expérience serait bonne pour elle, surtout que ce n'est que pour quatre-vingt-dix minutes par semaine.

A cette école ils jouent dehors l'après-midi ou font du sport; ce n'est pas vraiment l'école, mais ces activités font partie du programme de l'école. Il est clair pour moi que ma fille n'ira pas à l'école pour toute la semaine ou même toute la journée, et elle continuera à y aller seulement si elle aime bien. Je peux aussi imaginer qu'elle n'y aille pas. Pour elle, ça dépend de son besoin de contact avec d'autres enfants étant donné qu'à la maison elle est très seule.

Voilà comment nous vivons en famille et pourquoi je pense que la façon dont les enfants apprennent n'est pas importante. Parfois je me demande si mon fils va manquer quelque chose en n'allant pas à l'école. Quand j'y pense avec réalisme, je me rends compte qu'il ne manque rien. Parfois nous en parlons et je lui demande s'il aimerait essayer ceci ou cela (par exemple, suivre un programme quelconque). La plupart du temps il me dit: "Non, je fais les choses qui m'intéressent personnellement." Cela ne l'intéresse pas de suivre un programme scolaire, d'apprendre avec un ordinateur ou de suivre un cours à distance.

L'été dernier aurait été sa quatrième année à l'école. La quatrième année en Allemagne est la dernière année de l'école primaire. Les autorités scolaires ont demandé si elles pouvaient le tester et je leur ai dit qu'il ne suivait pas de curriculum, que je ne l'instruisais en rien. Quand les autorités scolaires ont compris notre méthode, ils ont décidé de lui faire passer un test oral. Il a eu de très très bons résultats. Ils étaient étonnés. Ils lui ont offert une place dans une école de haut niveau (en Allemagne ça s'appelle 'Gymnasium'). Ils ont offert de le laisser aller au 'Gymnasium' sans tests supplémentaires; normalement ils font faire des examens d'entrée. Nous y avons réfléchi et immédiatement j'ai eu le sentiment que ce n'était pas une bonne idée parce qu'il est encore trop jeune. Cela détruirait tout s'il y allait tous les jours. Alors j'ai dit à la responsable à l'administration scolaire que ce n'était pas possible.

Ensuite elle a offert de le laisser participer à des cours qui l'intéressaient comme l'art, l'anglais ou l'allemand ou d'autres cours qu'il pouvait choisir. Alors nous y avons réfléchi et un autre été est en train d'arriver et il est encore à la maison et n'est pas allé à l'école même pour quelques cours. Je pense que c'était une bonne décision de ne pas y aller. J'ai l'impression que s'il commençait à être assis dans une classe de trente élèves et suivre un cours de quarante-cinq minutes et entendre tout d'un enseignant et voir tout sur un tableau, alors il perdrait quelque chose.

Mécontentement avec les écoles

Les Allemands retirent leurs enfants de l'école parce qu'ils sont mécontents des écoles, comme dans d'autres pays européens. Il y a environ un mois, j'ai rencontré une femme qui avait retiré son fils de l'école. Son fils a maintenant dix-sept ans donc ça s'est passé il y a longtemps. Elle l'a retiré de l'école parce qu'il avait eu tant de problèmes. Malgré le fait qu'elle avait tellement essayé de trouver un moyen pour qu'il puisse rester à l'école, ce n'était tout simplement pas possible. Elle a été obligée de retirer son fils de l'école car c'était le seul moyen d'arrêter sa souffrance et puis, ils ont voyagé à travers l'Europe. Elle a quitté le pays pour éviter d'avoir des problèmes légaux et politiques. Elle m'a dit qu'elle a été obligée d'instruire son fils à la maison, sans quoi il n'aurait rien appris. Elle l'a instruit selon la méthode 'école-à-la-maison' mais pas pour des raisons religieuses.

Je pense qu'il doit y avoir d'autres familles comme celle-ci, mais normalement on ne les connaît pas parce qu'elles se cachent. Même maintenant, la femme avec qui j'ai parlé m'a dit qu'elle n'aimerait pas donner son numéro de téléphone à qui que ce soit ou être connue avant l'année prochaine, lorsque son fils aura dix-huit ans. Elle ne veut pas de problèmes.

Je ne connais que quelques familles du groupe d'instruction en famille dont les enfants ne sont jamais allés à l'école, même au début. La plupart des familles ont retiré leurs enfants de l'école parce qu'elles ont vécu de mauvaises expériences et rencontré d'autres enfants qui étaient instruits à domicile. Une famille avait des enfants en quatrième et en deuxième année quand les parents ont décidé de les retirer de l'école. Certains parents instructeurs informels ont retiré leurs enfants de l'école parce que les enfants eux-mêmes refusaient tout simplement d'y aller.

Mon fils avait huit ans lorsqu'il quitta l'école. Et bien qu'il m'ait dit qu'il n'aimait pas aller à l'école et qu'il voulait arrêter, si je lui avais dit "Non, il faut que tu y ailles", il y aurait été, j'en suis sûre. C'était plutôt ma décision. Je voulais mettre fin à la situation parce qu'il devenait un peu malade à l'école. Nous étions tous fous à la maison à cause de l'école.

Je pense que beaucoup d'enfants deviennent malades à l'école et la plupart des parents les forcent à y aller quand même. S'ils ne sont pas en état d'y aller, les parents leur donnent des médicaments. Seulement peu d'entre eux remettent en question la fréquentation scolaire et permettent à leurs enfants de rester à la maison au moins pour une durée passagère. Justement hier, sur notre liste de discussion internet, une femme a écrit qu'elle prenait soin d'un enfant qui avait arrêté d'aller à l'école parce qu'il y avait trop souffert. Il y avait tellement souffert que les autorités scolaires l'avaient autorisé à ne plus y aller et la famille n'avait pas été sanctionnée. Parfois on entend parler de cas tels que celui-ci, mais la majorité des familles qui retirent leurs enfants de l'école sont susceptibles d'avoir des problèmes juridiques et c'est pour cela que parfois elles se cachent.

Et si mon enfant veut aller à l'école...
En tant qu'instructrice non-scolaire, que ferais-je si mon fils voulait aller à l'école, me demandez-vous ? Je lui dirais ceci : "Si tu es capable de te lever le matin tout seul, d'entendre le réveil, et si tu es capable de tout préparer tout seul, tu peux y aller. Moi, je ne vais rien faire pour te faire te lever." Je dois crier au moins dix fois pour faire lever mon fils, voyez-vous, parce qu'il dort profondément. S'il pouvait se lever tout seul, ça irait. Maintenant qu'il a onze ans je pense qu'il est possible qu'il veuille un jour aller à l'école parce qu'il est volontairement académique. Il aime être comme les autres ; donc il est possible qu'il aille à l'école.

Mais je pense que s'il va à l'école, après avoir pu faire tout tout seul à la maison, après deux semaines il verra que l'école c'est une grande pagaille. Il verra qu'il n'en tirera rien de bon. Je crois qu'il reconnaîtra très rapidement qu'il ne profitera pas d'un enseignement scolaire parce qu'il est déjà habitué à mener ses propres projets et à vivre à son rythme à lui. Je crois que trouver son propre rythme est très important. Le problème est que l'école divise les sujets en petits cours : quarante-cinq minutes de maths, quarante-cinq minutes d'allemand – cela n'a aucun sens. Il n'est possible de se soumettre à cette bêtise que si on veut accomplir quelque chose de précis, par exemple tel ou tel métier.

Le futur
Si mon fils veut faire une carrière dans quelque chose de précis, par exemple s'il veut travailler comme artiste ou étudier la physique, nous devrons lui trouver un lieu où il pourra travailler avec quelqu'un sur ces sujets. C'est seulement de cette manière qu'il pourra, je pense, s'adapter à un autre rythme,

parce qu'il verra dans ce cas que ce rythme est bénéfique. Il y a une grande différence entre ceci et l'école où tout est artificiel. On peut apprendre à vivre à un rythme différent si on est avec quelqu'un qui vit sa vie en faisant ce qu'il veut faire. Même si on fait un travail dur, si c'est un travail qu'on a choisi de faire (ou même qu'on est amené à faire dans la vie) et lorsqu'il est possible de voir un **sens** dans la réalisation de ce travail, on peut apprendre à vivre à un autre rythme.

Das Leben ohne Schule in Deutschland

von Stefanie Mohsennia

Stefanie Mohsennia ist Bibliothekarin, Mutter eines unbeschulten Sohnes, Autorin des Buches 'Schulfrei : Lernen ohne Grenzen' und Webmaster des 'Informationszentrum Leben ohne Schule', welches Artikel, Gesetzesregelungen, Bücher, Links und Termine rund um das Leben ohne Schule bietet.

Mehr als 65 Jahre nachdem Hitler 1939 den Schulzwang eingeführt hat, ist das Leben ohne Schule in Deutschland bis zum heutigen Tag keine legale Bildungsoption. Dennoch ist das Leben ohne Schule in Deutschland Realität. Es gibt eine wachsende Gemeinschaft von Familien, deren Kinder zu Hause lernen – die Schätzungen reichen von 500 bis zu 3.000 Kindern.

Die meisten Familien, deren Kinder nicht beschult werden, lassen sich zwei Hauptgruppen zuordnen. Ein beträchtlicher Prozentsatz der Familien, die ihre Kinder zu Hause unterrichten, hat sich aus religiösen Gründen dafür entschieden. Diese Familien profitieren von der tatkräftigen Unterstützung durch 'Schulunterricht zu Hause e.V.' (Schuzh), einer nationalen Organisation, die der amerikanischen 'Home School Legal Defense Association' (HSLDA) angegliedert ist und rechtliche Beratung in Sachen Hausunterricht anbietet. Oft unterrichten die christlichen Familien nach dem 'Schule zu Hause'-Stil und melden ihre Kinder bei einer Fernschule an. Eine Reihe von Familien ist bei der 'Deutschen Fernschule' (df) eingeschrieben, der einzigen offiziell anerkannten deutschen Fernschule, die ihre Dienste jedoch nicht in der Bundesrepublik Deutschland ansässigen Familien anbieten soll, sondern Missionars- oder Diplomatenfamilien im Ausland. Andere Familien sind in der 'Philadelphia-

119

Schule' eingeschrieben, einer christlichen Fernschule, die zurzeit rund 300 Schüler aus ganz Deutschland betreut und seit 25 Jahren ohne Genehmigung der deutschen Schulbehörden betrieben wird.

Die Befürworter des selbst bestimmten Lernens bilden eine weitere große Gruppe. Diese Familien vertrauen darauf, dass ihre Kinder fähig sind aus eigenem Antrieb zu lernen, was auch immer sie brauchen. Sie setzen auf informelles, kindzentriertes, interessenbasiertes Lernen. Das selbst bestimmte Lernen ist allerdings eine noch recht junge Bewegung in Deutschland. Mehr und mehr Eltern schlagen den Weg des natürlichen Lernens ein und allmählich bauen die Familien Kontakte zu Gleichgesinnten auf. Regelmäßige Treffen auf lokaler Ebene gibt es bisher nur sehr vereinzelt, da es noch nicht viele Familien mit unbeschulten Kindern gibt und sich die wenigen Familien über das ganze Land verteilen. Eine Gruppe von Eltern, deren Kinder keine Schule besuchen, hat in Süddeutschland vor kurzem begonnen, Ausflüge zu organisieren. Der 'Bundesverband Natürlich Lernen e.V.' (BVNL) organisiert nationale Treffen und ein Familien-Sommercamp, an denen im Durchschnitt zwischen 20 und 40 Familien teilnehmen. Eine Mailingliste und ein gedruckter Rundbrief, der von der 'Initiative für selbstbestimmtes Lernen' herausgegeben wird, dienen als Hauptkommunikationsmittel zwischen den Familien mit unbeschulten Kindern. Seit 2004 hat die 'Clonlara-Schule' aus Michigan in den USA ihre Dienste auf Deutschland ausgeweitet.

Langsam aber sicher beginnt sich das Phänomen 'Leben ohne Schule' in Deutschland zu verbreiten. Im Laufe der vergangenen Monate ist in den Medien häufiger über Familien mit unbeschulten Kindern berichtet worden. Zum Teil war die Berichterstattung neutral, teilweise sogar positiv.

Während des Kasseler Expertentreffens im Januar 2006 wurden besprochen, wie sich die Familien mit unbeschulten Kindern in Zukunft stärker untereinander vernetzten können und wie man die Bewegung besser organisieren kann.

© Stefanie Mohsennia, 2006

Bildung zu Hause und selbstbestimmtes Lernen: Ein Beispiel aus Deutschland

von Elisabeth Kuhnle

Elisabeth Kuhnle ist Mutter eines elfjährigen Jungen und eines achtjährigen Mädchens, die beide ohne Schule leben und lernen. Sie lebt in Karlsruhe, Deutschland, und hat drei Jahre Erfahrung mit dem Leben ohne Schule. Sie berichtete uns auf Englisch.

'Bildung zu Hause' in Deutschland

In Deutschland haben wir aus zwei Gründen eine besondere Situation. Erstens ist Bildung zu Hause illegal. Zweitens entscheiden sich die meisten Familien aus religiösen Gründen für eine Bildung ihrer Kinder zu Hause; diese Familien praktizieren meist Hausunterricht. Informelles Lernen (das ich 'Lernen ohne Unterweisung', nenne) ist bei uns ein sehr junges Phänomen. Nur wenige Familien, die ohne Schule leben, lassen ihre Kinder ganz frei – ohne Unterweisung – lernen. Diese Familien sind über ganz Deutschland verteilt, so daß es nur wenig Gelegenheit gibt, um sich zusammenzutun. Nähere Kontakte bestehen eigentlich nur zwischen einzelnen Familien. Es gibt noch kein bundesweites Netzwerk für uns. Wie ich mit meinen Kindern lebe, wird von unserer spezifisch deutschen Situation beeinflußt.

Das vorerst wichtigste Ziel, wofür wir uns hier in Deutschland einsetzen sollten, ist, den Menschen zu vermitteln, daß es sowas wie 'Homeschooling', Bildung zu Hause, Lernen ohne Schule überhaupt gibt. Die meisten Leute haben keine Ahnung davon, daß es Kinder gibt, die nicht in die Schule gehen, sondern zu Hause lernen. Oft ist die Tatsache, daß es 'Homeschooling' überhaupt gibt, nicht einmal Lehrern und Schulräten bekannt.

Ich glaube, daß es viele Familien mit kleineren Kindern, die noch nicht schulpflichtig sind, gibt, die von informellem (natürlichem) Lernen überzeugt sind und 'Familie' positiv sehen (positiver als die Menschen meiner Generation), und die sich deshalb für ein Leben ohne Schule interessieren. Erst einmal schicken sie ihre Kinder nicht in den Kindergarten. Dies ist für viele Familien ein erster Schritt, 'Nein' zum System zu sagen.

Sich mit Gleichgesinnten vernetzen

Wie gesagt, Menschen die sich hier für informelles Lernen interessieren, haben noch kein richtiges Netzwerk. Während es seit fast zwanzig Jahren eine größere Anzahl religiöser Heimschul-Familien und Familien-Zusammenschlüsse gibt, haben diejenigen, die natürliches bzw. informelles Lernen bevorzugen, erst vor zwei oder drei Jahren begonnen, sich zu organisieren. Wir fangen gerade erst an, unsere Netzwerke zu bilden, und das ist nicht einfach.

Zwei Familien aus der Gegend von Heidelberg und aus Mannheim, beides nicht weit von uns entfernt, treffen wir öfter. Eine davon begann das 'Homeschooling' mit klassischem Hausunterricht. Dann haben sie gemerkt, daß klassischer Hausunterricht nicht wirklich gut für ihre Kinder war, und sie ließen den Kindern nach und nach mehr Freiheiten (beim Lernen). Darin zeigt sich, daß Eltern von den Reaktionen ihrer Kinder lernen. Zusätzlich haben Menschen bzw. Familien mit unterschiedlichen Ansichten die Gelegenheit, über diese zu diskutieren, wenn sie sich treffen; sie können sich darüber austauschen, was sie über ihr Leben neu erfahren, und was sie bei ihren Kindern beobachten. Dieser Austausch mag Eltern helfen, die Art und Weise, wie sie mit ihren Kindern umgehen, zu ändern. Diese Art von Austausch interessiert mich sehr. Daher bin ich momentan besonders daran interessiert, Familien, die zwar eventuell unterschiedliche Weltanschauungen haben, aber nicht zu weit von uns entfernt leben, zu treffen.

Außerdem habe ich 'Les Enfants D'Abord', einen französischen Verein, der alle Arten von 'Homeschoolern' vereint, kennengelernt und bin dort Mitglied geworden. Einmal im Monat fahren wir nach Straßburg zu einem Treffen im Haus einer anderen Mitgliedsfamilie. Die Kinder dieser Familie sind 'Unschooler'. Es war sehr wichtig für mich, französische 'Homeschool'-Familien kennenzulernen, da viele französische Familien Kinder haben, die niemals in ihrem Leben oder zumindestens über einen längeren Zeitraum nicht zur Schule gingen. Die Familien in diesem Verein haben die unterschiedlichsten Bildungs-erfahrungen mit ihren Kindern: manche Kinder waren in der Schule und haben sie verlassen, andere waren ursprünglich zu Hause und gingen dann später in eine Schule, manche waren nie in der Schule. Es gibt 'Unschooler' und andere, die zu Hause unterrichtet werden, einfach alles. Das ist interessant und wichtig zu erleben.

Erkenntnisse über das freie Lernen ohne Unterweisung

Zur Zeit mögen meine Kinder und ich es sehr gerne, wenn wir uns mit anderen Familien treffen, deren Kinder nicht zur Schule gehen. Wir treffen gerne Familien, die diese Erfahrung haben und interessante und schöne Sachen zusammen machen. Vor zwei Wochen machten wir eine Exkursion in die Gegend nördlich von Frankfurt, um die 'Saalburg' zu besichtigen. Das ist eine der Festungen, welche die Römer zur Sicherung des 'Limes' erbaut hatten. Wer wollte, konnte an einer Führung – speziell für Kinder geeignet – durch die verschiedenen Gebäude der Saalburg teilnehmen. Außerdem hatte eine der Mütter ein paar Angebote vorbereitet – zum Beispiel die Anfertigung einfacher Ledersandalen –, an denen sich die Kinder, wenn sie Lust hatten, beteiligen konnten. Dann machten wir einen Spaziergang durch diese Festung und ein bißchen weiter, um die gesamte Anlage herum, und ich, als Erwachsene, konnte spüren, wie es ist, wenn man an einen (geschichtsträchtigen) Ort kommt und die Dinge **empfinden** kann. Man lernt nicht nur aus einem Buch oder von dem, was ein Lehrer erzählt. Man ist dort, wo sich Geschichte ereignete, und kann den Dingen nachspüren. Und selbst wenn man diese Exkursion längst vergessen haben wird, wird dieses Gefühl, dieses Gespür – so denke ich – in einem geblieben sein, viel länger als längst vergessene Worte.

Aus solch kleinen Ereignissen lerne ich, wie Lernen durch und für mich selber funktioniert. Ich verstehe immer mehr, was "informelles Lernen" – Lernen ohne Unterweisung und in realen Zusammenhängen – bedeutet, und wie es abläuft. Zum Beispiel hat mir mein inzwischen elfjähriger Sohn vor etwa eineinhalb Jahren gesagt: "Ich will gerne Englisch und Französisch lernen." Aber er hatte nicht wirklich Lust, irgendeinen Kurs dafür zu besuchen. Manchmal sagte er: "Ja, ich möchte gerne einen Kurs mitmachen." und dann wieder hatte er doch keine Lust dazu. Vor wenigen Tagen – er war gerade in einem anderen Zimmer als ich – hörte ich, wie er einen englischen Satz vor sich hin sprach. Dieser Satz war nicht 'korrekt', doch immerhin ...; ich fragte ihn, woher er wohl die englischen Worte wußte? Er hat sie sich irgendwie angeeignet, sie aufgeschnappt, vielleicht in Liedtexten, oder auf dem Computer, ich weiß es auch nicht genau, aber diese Beobachtung war sehr interessant. Und das ist es, was ich bereits bei der Exkursion zur Saalburg gemerkt hatte: Wenn man sich innerhalb der Dinge (der wirklichen Welt, des echten Lebens) befindet, und wenn Lernen ein (integraler) Teil des Lebens ist, dann lernt man durch 'Hineinfühlen', obwohl ich mir nicht ganz sicher bin, ob dieser Ausdruck vermittelt, was ich meine.

Meine Tochter ist behindert. Hätte ich keine behinderte Tochter, würde mein Sohn vermutlich in die Schule gehen. Aber durch meine Tochter erkannte ich, daß es keinen (Rechtfertigungs-)Grund gibt, irgendetwas in ein Kind 'einzutrichtern'. Das Kind wird geboren, und alles, was dieses Kind mitbringt, wird sich zur passenden Zeit entfalten. Genauer gesagt: Kinder wissen und zeigen von sich aus, wann sie bereit sind, neue Fertigkeiten zu entwickeln und neue Kenntnisse aufzunehmen. In einem gewissen Sinn hat mir meine Tochter offenbart, wie Lernen vor sich geht.

Je mehr ich über Lernen und Schule und all diese Dinge nachdenke, desto mehr komme ich zu dem Schluß, daß es nicht nötig ist, über das Lernen nachzudenken und zu diskutieren. Es ist eigentlich nicht das Lernen, worauf wir uns konzentrieren sollten, da lernen sowieso integraler Bestandteil unseres Lebens ist. Es sollte uns möglich sein, uns auf andere Dinge zu konzentrieren. Wir müssen jedoch über das Lernen diskutieren, weil die Schulbehörden der Meinung sind, daß wir unsere Kinder in die Schule schicken müssen (damit sie – angeblich – überhaupt etwas lernen). Das ist meines Erachtens der einzige Grund dafür, warum wir über das Lernen und darüber, wie es funktioniert, diskutieren müssen, weil die Schulbehörden sich so verhalten, als ob man nur durch den Unterricht in Schulen lernen würde.

Insgesamt denke ich, daß das kein deutsches Phänomen ist, sondern eines, das typisch für alle sogenannten Industrienationen ist. Wissenschaftler versuchen herauszufinden, wie das Gehirn funktioniert, wie es lernt. Zu diesem Zweck dringen sie in Gehirne ein; sie dringen in Menschen ein. Alles wird von ihnen fein säuberlich auseinandergenommen. Wenn die Wissenschaftler und die Gesellschaft nur zu dem Zweck so vorgingen um zu erfahren, wie wir lernen, könnte ich dem, was sie machen, zustimmen. Es ist jedoch so, daß diese Forschungen darauf zielen herauszufinden, wie Menschen besser funktionieren, mit welchen Lernprogrammen man mehr aus ihnen herausholen kann. Das lehne ich entschieden ab. Es steht niemandem zu, sich Gedanken darüber zu machen, auf welche Weise ein anderer Mensch besser funktionieren könnte. Ich bin mir nicht ganz sicher, ob 'funktionieren' ausdrückt, was ich meine, aber es ist einfach nicht richtig, darüber nachzudenken, wie man einen anderen Menschen verbessern könnte, denn der andere Mensch trägt alles, was ihn ausmacht, bereits in sich. Daher denke ich auch, daß niemand das Recht hat, für andere Personen Programme auszuarbeiten. Niemand hat das Recht, für andere zu denken. Das einzige, was wir machen können und dürfen, ist, andere Menschen dabei zu begleiten, wenn sie in lebendigen Zusammenhängen lernen.

Das ist momentan mein Interesse hier in Deutschland: Leute zu finden, mit denen ich diese Gedanken austauschen kann, und mit ihnen zusammenzuarbeiten. Wir haben eine Mailingliste, um über solche Themen zu diskutieren, und wir haben daran gedacht, einmal eine Zeitschrift herauszubringen.

Unsere Familie

Für mich ist es eine gute Möglichkeit, mich mit der Theorie und Ideologie von Lernen und Schule auseinanderzusetzen, aber meine Kinder leben einfach ihr Leben zu Hause. Sie haben natürlich auch viele Kontakte nach außerhalb. Mein Sohn geht zum Beispiel in eine Musikschule. Er wollte schon lange unheimlich gerne Harfe spielen lernen, und wir haben lange darüber nachgedacht, welche Möglichkeiten es dafür gäbe, und nun hat er sich entschieden, in die Musikschule zu gehen. Er geht auch zu verschiedenen Bastel- und Werkkursen und trifft sich mit Freunden. Er ist sehr unabhängig, nicht nur was das Lernen betrifft, sondern er fährt auch ganz selbständig in der Gegend herum.

Mit meiner Tochter gehe ich zu verschiedenen Therapien. Ich halte es nicht für unbedingt nötig, aber wir haben sehr gute Therapeuten gefunden, und meine Tochter mag sie gerne, und deswegen gehen wir da hin. Vor einigen Wochen begannen wir, einmal wöchentlich nachmittags in eine Schule zu gehen; es ist eine Schule für geistig behinderte Kinder und Jugendliche. Meine Tochter geht in eine Gruppe mit sechs anderen Kindern in ihrem Alter, sie sind sieben bis acht Jahre alt, und zwar geht sie nur einmal nachmittags für eineinhalb Stunden dorthin.

Mein Sohn war eineinhalb Jahre in der Schule, er weiß also, was Schule ist. Er ging in die Schule, da ich damals nicht wußte, daß es überhaupt möglich ist, die Kinder zu Hause (lernen) zu lassen. Inzwischen geht also meine Tochter ein kleines bißchen in die Schule und sie mag es, dort andere Kinder zu treffen, was ansonsten aufgrund ihrer Behinderung sehr schwierig für sie ist. Ein weiterer Grund dafür, daß ich sie zur Schule bringe, ist, daß es die Schul- und Jugendämter gerne sehen, wenn man mit ihnen zusammenarbeitet. Sie mögen es, wenn man sich wenigstens anschaut, was sie anzubieten haben. Ich dachte mir, wenn meine Tochter gerne hingeht, wird diese Erfahrung gut für sie sein – und außerdem ist es ja nur für neunzig Minuten pro Woche.

In dieser Schule gehen sie am Nachmittag viel nach draußen und spielen oder sie machen Sport; es ist nicht so, wie man sich Schule (Unterricht) vorstellt, aber es ist ein Teil des Lehrplanes dieser Schule. Für mich steht fest, daß meine Tochter niemals die ganze Woche in die Schule gehen würde, noch nicht einmal einen ganzen Tag, und sie wird überhaupt nur dann weiter dorthin gehen, wenn sie es auch möchte. Ich kann mir auch gut vorstellen, daß sie gar nicht in die Schule geht. Für sie hängt der Schulbesuch auch damit zusammen, daß sie sehr gerne andere Kinder trifft, denn daheim ist sie oft recht alleine.

So leben wir als Familie, und wie die Kinder lernen, spielt eigentlich keine Rolle. Manchmal frage ich mich, ob mein Sohn dadurch, daß er nicht in die Schule geht, irgendetwas versäumt. Wenn ich wirklich klar und nüchtern darüber nachdenke, erkenne ich, daß er nichts versäumt. Manchmal unterhalten wir uns über dieses Thema und dann frage ich ihn, ob er dieses oder jenes (zum Beispiel in einem Kurs) ausprobieren möchte. Meistens antwortet er mir: "Nein, ich beschäftige mich lieber selber." Er hatte bis jetzt kein Interesse, ein Unterrichtsprogramm mitzumachen, oder mit Lernsoftware oder einem Fernschulprogramm zu lernen.

Letzten Sommer hätte er sein viertes Schuljahr abgeschlossen. Mit der vierten Klasse endet in Deutschland die Grundschulzeit. Vom Schulamt kam der Wunsch, daß er einen Test machen solle, und ich erklärte den zuständigen Personen, daß mein Sohn keinerlei Unterrichtsprogramm verfolgt. Ich unterrichte ihn überhaupt nicht. Als die Schulrätin, mit der ich sprach, dies verstand, entschied sie, daß mein Sohn einen mündlichen Test machen solle. Er hat diesen Test mit äußerst guten Ergebnissen bestanden. Das überraschte alle. Die Schulrätin empfahl meinem Sohn, auf ein Gymnasium zu gehen. Sie bot ihm an, daß er ohne weitere Aufnahmeprüfung auf das Gymnasium gehen könne (normalerweise hätte er dafür eine Aufnahmeprüfung bestehen müssen, weil er ja kein Übergangszeugnis hatte). Wir haben über dieses (verlockende) Angebot nachgedacht, und sofort hatte ich das Gefühl, daß dies keine so gute Idee ist, weil mein Sohn noch zu jung dafür ist. Es würde alles Bisherige zerstören, wenn er nun jeden Tag in die Schule ginge. Daher sagte ich der Schulrätin, daß ein Besuch des Gymnasiums nicht in Frage käme.

Daraufhin bot sie ihm an, daß er nur einige wenige, ausgewählte Fächer besuchen könne, die er gerne machen würde, zum Beispiel Kunst, Englisch, Deutsch oder andere Fächer, die er auswählen könne. Wir haben lange darüber nachgedacht, bis vor kurzem – fast einen Sommer später, und er ist immer noch zu Hause und hat auch nicht für einige wenige, ausgewählte Fächer die Schule besucht. Ich glaube, daß es die richtige Entscheidung war, nicht in die Schule zu gehen. Ich habe den Eindruck, daß er etwas verlieren würde, wenn er anfinge, in einem Klassenzimmer mit dreißig Mitschülern zu sitzen und alles in 45-Minuten-Einheiten zu lernen, alles von einem Lehrer zu hören und alles auf einer Tafel zu sehen.

Von der Schule enttäuscht

Deutsche nehmen ihre Kinder aus der Schule heraus, weil sie von der Schule enttäuscht sind, wie das auch in anderen europäischen Ländern der Fall ist. Vor etwa einem Monat traf ich eine Frau, die ihren Sohn aus der Schule herausgenommen hatte; der Sohn ist allerdings inzwischen siebzehn Jahre alt, das liegt also schon eine Weile zurück. Sie hat ihn aus der Schule genommen, weil er dort so viele Schwierigkeiten gehabt hatte. Obwohl sie sich sehr bemüht hatte, einen Weg zu finden, damit er in der Schule bleiben könne, gelang es ihr nicht – es war unmöglich. Sie war regelrecht dazu gezwungen, ihren Sohn aus der Schule herauszunehmen, denn das war der einzige Weg, um sein Leiden dort zu beenden, und dann begann sie, mit ihm durch Europa zu reisen. Sie verließ das Land, um rechtliche und politische Probleme zu vermeiden. Sie erzählte mir, daß sie ihren Sohn zu Hause unterrichten mußte, sonst hätte er niemals etwas gelernt. Sie hat ihrem Sohn zu Hause richtigen Unterricht gegeben, allerdings nicht aus religiösen Gründen.

Ich denke, daß es noch mehr solcher Familien geben muß, doch normalerweise erfährt man nicht von ihnen, da sie sich (bzw. die Tatsache, daß die Kinder nicht in die Schule gehen) versteckt halten. Auch die Frau, von der ich eben erzählte, sagte mir, daß sie niemandem ihre Telefonnummer geben oder irgendwie bekannt werden möchte, bevor nicht ihr Sohn im nächsten Jahr achtzehn (und damit volljährig) wäre. Sie wollte jeglichen Ärger vermeiden.

Ich kenne nur wenige Familien aus dem Kreis der deutschen 'Homeschooler', deren Kinder niemals (auch nicht anfänglich) in die Schule gingen. Die meisten Familien haben ihre Kinder aus der Schule herausgenommen, weil sie dort schlechte Erfahrungen gemacht hatten und weil sie andere Kinder, die zu Hause lernen, kennengelernt hatten. Die Kinder einer Familie, an die ich mich erinnere, waren in der vierten und in der zweiten Klasse, als die Eltern sie aus der Schule nahmen. Einige Eltern, die dem Prinzip des 'Unschooling' nahe stehen, haben ihre Kinder aus der Schule herausgenommen, weil die Kinder von sich aus einen weiteren Schulbesuch schlichtweg verweigerten.

Mein Sohn war acht Jahre alt, als er die Schule verließ. Und obwohl er mir selbst gesagt hatte, daß ihm die Schule keinen Spaß mache und daß er nicht mehr hingehen wolle, – wenn ich zu ihm gesagt hätte: "Das gibt's nicht. Du mußt hingehen!" – wäre er weiter hingegangen, da bin ich mir sicher. Es war zuerst einmal und hauptsächlich meine Entscheidung. Ich wollte die Sache beenden, da die Schule (und der damit verbundene Zwang) ihn bereits etwas krank gemacht hatte. Wir waren zu Hause schon alle ganz verrückt wegen der Schule (und all dem damit verbundenen Drumherum).

Ich glaube, daß es viele Kinder gibt, die wegen der Schule krank werden, doch die Eltern zwingen sie, trotzdem hinzugehen. Wenn sie es so nicht mehr schaffen, in die Schule zu gehen, geben die Eltern ihnen Medikamente. Nur wenige kommen auf die Idee, die Schule in Frage zu stellen, und den Kindern zu erlauben, daß sie eine Weile zu Hause bleiben. Gestern erst hat eine Frau auf unserer Mailingliste davon berichtet, daß sie einmal ein Kind in Pflege genommen hatten. Dieser Junge verließ die Schule, weil er dort so sehr litt. Er litt sogar so sehr, daß selbst die Schulbehörden damit einverstanden waren, daß er nicht mehr hinging. Die Familie wurde nicht bestraft oder sonstwie unter Druck gesetzt. Manchmal hört man von solchen Fällen, meist jedoch ist es so, daß Familien, die ihre Kinder aus der Schule herausnehmen, Schwierigkeiten bekommen, und deswegen halten sich einige von ihnen versteckt.

Was wäre, wenn mein Kind in die Schule gehen wollte?
Sie fragen mich, was ich – als Anhängerin des selbstbestimmten und freien Lernens – machen würde, wenn mein Sohn in die Schule gehen will? Ich würde ihm folgendes sagen: "Wenn Du in der Lage bist, morgens selbständig aufzustehen, wenn es Dir gelingt, den Wecker zu hören, und wenn Du alles Notwendige selbst erledigen kannst, dann kannst Du gehen. Ich aber werde nicht mehr versuchen, Dich aufzuwecken." Ich mußte jeden Morgen mindestens zehnmal rufen, um meinen Sohn wach zu bekommen, verstehen Sie, denn er hat einen sehr tiefen Schlaf. Wenn er von sich aus aufwachen und sich fertigmachen würde, wäre es in Ordnung. Ich denke, daß er – nachdem er mittlerweile elf Jahre alt ist – möglicherweise bald äußern wird, daß er in die Schule gehen will, da er eine Neigung zu wissenschaftlichem Arbeiten hat. Und er möchte gerne normal sein. Daher ist es schon möglich, daß er von sich aus in die Schule gehen wird.

Aber ich stelle mir auch vor, daß er – sobald er in die Schule gehen wird – nach vielleicht zwei Wochen schon erkennen wird, daß die Schule ein großer

Reinfall ist – nachdem er zuvor in der Lage war, daheim alles ganz selbständig zu machen. Er würde es merken, wenn er nichts wirklich Sinnvolles in der Schule mitbekäme. Ich glaube, er würde schnell merken, daß das schulische Lernen ihm nichts bringt, denn er ist ja bereits gewohnt, seine eigenen Pläne zu machen und nach seinem eigenen Rhythmus zu leben. Ich denke, daß es sehr wichtig ist, einen eigenen Rhythmus zu finden. Das Problem der Schule ist, daß die Fächer dort in kleine Einheiten aufgeteilt werden: eine Stunde Mathe, eine Stunde Deutsch – das ist Unsinn. Solch einem Unsinn kann man sich nur dann fügen, wenn man wirklich etwas ganz Bestimmtes machen will, zum Beispiel, wenn man einen bestimmten Beruf erlernen möchte.

Zukunftsaussichten
Wenn mein Sohn sich in einer bestimmten Sparte vervollkommnen möchte, sagen wir mal, falls er als Künstler arbeiten möchte oder falls er Physik studieren möchte, müßten wir einen Ort finden, wo er mit jemandem zusammen auf diesen Gebieten arbeiten kann. Nur so, denke ich, könnte er sich einem anderen Rhythmus anpassen, da er erkennen würde, daß diese Veränderung ihm einen Nutzen bringt. Es liegt ein großer Unterschied zwischen dem, was ich hier meine, und der Schule, wo alles künstlich ist. Man kann lernen, nach einem 'fremden' Rhythmus zu leben, wenn man mit jemandem zusammenkommt, der sein Leben so lebt, daß das, was er macht, ihn erfüllt. Selbst wenn es harte Arbeit ist, aber eine Arbeit, die man selbst gewählt hat und die einem vor allem **sinnvoll** erscheint (oder vielleicht selbst dann, wenn es das Leben selbst war, das einem diesen Weg aufzeigte), dann kann man lernen, nach einem anderen Rhythmus zu leben.

Home Education in Switzerland

In Switzerland, the Code Civil Suisse of 10 December 1907 puts the onus for ensuring that a child is educated, including their physical, intellectual and moral well-being, onto the parents. Laws governing the education of children in Switzerland vary between the 26 cantons, and are enforced at a local level (Marti Hanna, 1991, Enquete suisse sur le homeschooling, Endlich/enfin, No.2.). Some cantons are sympathetic to home education, while in others state schooling is compulsory. Quite a few cantons have changed their school laws in the past couple of years and made the laws concerning privately educating a child at home much more strict. Restricting the freedom of parents to educate their children at home may be against the national constitution and laws; this has yet to be tested.

Educating children at home is still relatively uncommon. Families in remote farms, the circus, or other mobile occupations are **usually** allowed to do so, as are international families or those living in Switzerland temporarily. For Swiss and permanently resident families, permission must be obtained and documentation such as annual and/or weekly plans may be requested. An annual visit from a school official is fairly common.

Most children are required to be educated in one of the languages of the country (German, French, Italian or Romansch). If a child is to be educated in any other language, permission must be sought. The child will still be required to learn one of them, usually that of the canton in which they are residing, as a foreign language.

Home education is growing in Switzerland despite all the hurdles, with the highest concentrations of home educators in the cantons of Geneva, Bern and Zurich.

Home Education and Learner-Managed Learning: An example from Switzerland

by Coni Lagler

Coni Lagler, home educating mother of three children, spoke to us from Switzerland. She spoke in German.

Home Education in Switzerland

In Switzerland we have a school curriculum that is treated like the Holy Bible. So, if one home educates in the way that I do there is a fine line to be walked in order to avoid conflict with the authorities whilst still allowing one's child to develop in their own way. It is not possible everywhere, because the rules vary from county to county. There are counties in which our family 'project' would have had to be abandoned. There are counties where one has to be a qualified teacher, have a timetable like in a school and use teaching resources. In the county where I live, Zurich, there is going to be a referendum in June 2005, which may make home education impossible for all but qualified teachers.

I do not know the number of home educators in Switzerland. In Zürich County there are about 140 families who home educate. I know of a couple of them and they are Christian oriented. I don't have any contact with them because we have different life orientations. There is little tolerance or understanding regarding home education among the general public in Switzerland. It depends on the person, to whom I'm talking, but nowadays I seldom enter into a discussion. I explain what we do to those who are genuinely interested, if they ask. I do not keep the children home during school hours to avoid questions, though. It is entirely up to the children whether they go out or not.

As to how we have managed with the authorities, our situation is a little unusual, because after about a year and a half of home educating I got a job in a school where the children are treated in a similar manner to how they are at home. I was able to take the children with me. Because of this, the authorities left me in peace for a while. The school, based on Montessori and Rudolf Steiner influences, should have been very liberal. However, it didn't work out. The adults could never reach agreement.

The Swiss education authorities do visit home educators at home to inspect them. We are visited in the same way that a school is visited, twice a year. In my case this has gone relatively well, but not without some difficulties. In some places one can experience enormous problems. I usually explain my method as an 'extended Montessori philosophy'. We, the children and I, always decide beforehand, that during the two-hour visit by the authorities, the children will do some writing or work at the computer. Almost like a small theatre production. What the authorities would like of course is for us to show pieces of work to document what has been done and when! So far I have somehow managed without doing that.

Why I Began Home Educating
For me it is all about every child being his or her own person. Every child learns differently and every child has different interests. It is important to me that children can be full of life and that they can be at one with themselves, they can develop their sense of self and not have someone else telling them how they have to be and what they should be able to do. Children learn to walk when they are ready to. That is the way, I think, that all learning happens.

Everyone is an individual and has his or her own interests to develop. Everyone has his or her own aptitude and strength. Also, I think when everyone learns in a way that is right for them, or learns about whatever is right for them, then they can take *responsibility* for it. If at school they are told: "You must do this and that, in this way, with these results", then the children are not able to take responsibility, they can only fulfil something for someone else. They won't learn to take responsibility for their own lives.

Our Family
I have three children between thirteen and twenty-one years old. The eldest attended school for ten years in the normal way. My second child completed about half of the time and my third child only did just the beginning, the first year. I didn't find out until then that home education is an option in certain Swiss counties. Can I see differences among my children based on how long they were in school? This is difficult to determine! All three children are so different anyway. I notice the differences between the three children less than the *changes* in the children once they came out of school. Especially with my middle daughter, she used to cry, had a massive inferiority complex, and was really in despair until I found out that I could home educate. She is now a well-balanced and engaged person. I know other children who have been home

educated in a similar way, carefully accompanied in their learning and living from a younger age, who were given these opportunities earlier. I find these children to be much more open. They have their feet on the ground. They develop less negative behaviour patterns.

How We Home Educate – Informal Child-led Education

I just do my own thing really. I don't know how others do things. There are different styles of home education here in Switzerland. The majority, I suppose, are doing it for religious reasons, or they do 'school-at-home'. Here is a typical example from our family: When we began home educating my youngest could add up to 20. After the summer holidays, without anything particular happening or training during that time, he could suddenly add up to 100. I think he achieved this mainly through using money. He got to know money, counted it, sorted it, went shopping, and played with my purse. He simply *experienced* money. He quite naturally doesn't want to be cheated when he spends money; he doesn't want to pay too much and he wants to receive the right change.

With reading and writing it is much the same. There is so much writing everywhere and numbers are used all over the place. I suppose that in a dark room where there is nothing to learn, then nothing will be learned, well, at least none of these basic skills. But outside, in life, where all those skills are being used... in the same way that they learnt to walk, they will be able to read and calculate.

The Future

How would my two younger children deal with the world of work? Well, in my son's case I'll have to wait and see. My daughter has an apprentice position that she is determined to do, partly to show other people that it can be done, even without official school qualifications. She is not particularly enthusiastic about my philosophy. I don't think she yet appreciates the advantages that it has brought her. I think it has been good for her; she has become so full of life, although she used to be so insecure. I feel that she now has both feet firmly on the ground and that she will cope with the apprenticeship. She will definitely find her path in life.

L'instruction à la maison en Suisse

En Suisse, le Code civil suisse du 10 décembre 1907 donne aux parents la responsabilité de s'assurer de l'éducation de leurs enfants, y compris de leur bien-être physique, intellectuel et moral. Les lois qui régissent l'instruction des enfants en Suisse varient entre les 26 cantons. (Marti Hanna, 1991, *Enquête suisse sur le homeschooling*, Endlich/enfin, No.2). Certains cantons acceptent l'instruction à la maison tandis que dans d'autres, l'école est obligatoire. Plusieurs cantons ont changé leur législation sur l'école depuis deux ans et ont fait passer des lois plus strictes concernant l'instruction des enfants à domicile. Il se peut que l'atteinte à la liberté des parents d'instruire leurs enfants à la maison soit contraire à la constitution et aux lois nationales, mais cet argument n'a pas encore été testé devant les tribunaux.

L'instruction à la maison est encore peu courante. Les familles qui vivent dans des fermes isolées, qui font du cirque ou d'autres activités nécessitant des déplacements ont en général le droit de le faire, comme les familles internationales ou celles résidant temporairement en Suisse. Les familles suisses qui y résident de manière permanente doivent obtenir une autorisation, et les autorités peuvent demander un projet pédagogique écrit annuel et/ou hebdomadaire. Une visite annuelle d'un inspecteur scolaire est assez courante.

Concernant les langues, la plupart des enfants doivent étudier dans l'une des langues du pays (l'allemand, le français, l'italien ou le romanche). Pour instruire l'enfant dans une autre langue que celles-ci, on doit obtenir une autorisation. L'enfant sera en tout cas obligé d'apprendre comme langue étrangère l'une des langues du pays : en général, la langue du canton où il réside.

Pourtant, l'instruction à la maison prend de l'ampleur en Suisse, malgré toutes les difficultés à surmonter pour la pratiquer. Les plus grandes concentrations de familles instruisant leurs enfants à domicile se trouvent dans les cantons de Genève, de Berne et de Zurich.

Instruction en famille et apprentissage auto-géré : Un exemple de Suisse

par Coni Lagler

Coni Lagler, mère de trois enfants les instruisant à la maison, nous a parlé en allemand de la Suisse.

L'instruction à la maison en Suisse

En Suisse, nous avons un programme scolaire considéré comme la Bible. Donc, si quelqu'un pratique l'instruction en famille comme je le fais, il y a une mince frontière à respecter pour éviter les conflits avec les autorités afin qu'elles nous permettent de laisser l'enfant s'épanouir selon son schéma propre. Ce n'est pas possible partout parce que les lois varient d'un canton à l'autre.

Il y a des cantons dans lesquels nous aurions été obligés d'abandonner notre projet familial. Il y a des cantons où l'un des parents doit être un enseignant qualifié, avoir une organisation semblable à celle de l'école et utiliser des ressources scolaires. Dans le canton dans lequel je vis, Zurich, il est prévu un référendum en juin 2005 qui devrait ne rendre l'instruction en famille accessible qu'aux enseignants qualifiés.

Je ne connais pas le nombre de familles qui font l'instruction à la maison en Suisse. Dans le canton de Zurich il y a 140 familles environ qui pratiquent l'instruction en famille. J'en connais un certain nombre et ils sont Chrétiens pratiquants. Je n'ai pas de contact avec eux parce que nous avons des choix de vie différents.

En Suisse, beaucoup dans l'opinion publique, ne comprennent pas qu'on n'aille pas à l'école. Cela dépend de la personne avec qui je parle mais aujourd'hui, je développe peu souvent le sujet. J'explique ce que nous faisons à ceux qui sont sincèrement intéressés, s'ils le demandent. Je ne garde pourtant pas les enfants à la maison pendant le temps scolaire pour éviter les questions. C'est aux enfants de choisir s'ils veulent sortir ou pas.

Notre situation est quelque peu inhabituelle vis à vis des autorités. Après un an et demi d'instruction à la maison, j'ai eu un emploi dans une école où les enfants étaient traités d'une manière similaire à celle avec laquelle ils l'étaient à la maison. J'étais autorisée à emmener les enfants avec moi. Grâce à ça, les autorités m'ont laissée tranquille pendant un temps. L'école, qui s'inspirait des méthodes Montessori et Rudolph Steiner, aurait dû être très ouverte. Cependant, cela n'a pas marché. Les adultes n'ont jamais pu s'entendre.

Les inspecteurs suisses se rendent au domicile des parents qui font l'instruction à la maison. Nous sommes inspectés de la même manière qu'une école, deux fois par an. Dans mon cas, ça s'est relativement bien passé, mais pas sans difficultés. À certains endroits, on peut rencontrer de sérieux problèmes.

Je définis en général ma méthode comme une "extension de la philosophie Montessorienne". Nous - les enfants et moi-même, décidons au préalable ce qu'ils écriront durant la visite de deux heures des inspecteurs, ou s'ils travailleront à l'ordinateur. À peu près comme une petite production théâtrale. Les inspecteurs voudraient bien que nous leur présentions des traces écrites indiquant de ce qui a été fait et quand ! Jusqu'à présent, d'une manière ou d'une autre, j'ai réussi à contourner cette demande.

Pourquoi j'ai commencé l'instruction à la maison

Pour moi, tout part de ce que chaque enfant est une personne distincte. Chaque enfant apprend différemment et chaque enfant a différents centres d'intérêts. Il est important pour moi que les enfants soient pleins de vie et qu'ils puissent être eux-mêmes, qu'ils puissent développer leur conscience de soi et non pas que quelqu'un d'autre leur dise comment ils doivent être et ce qu'ils doivent faire. Les enfants apprennent à marcher quand ils sont prêts à le faire. C'est ainsi, je pense, que chaque apprentissage se fait.

Chacun est particulier et a ses propres intérêts à épanouir. Chacun a sa propre aptitude et sa propre force. Aussi, je pense que lorsque quelqu'un apprend de la manière qui lui convient ou qu'il apprend ce qui est bon pour lui, alors il peut en prendre la **responsabilité**. Quand, à l'école, il est dit : " Tu dois faire ci et ça, de cette manière, avec ce résultat ", alors les enfants ne sont pas autorisés à prendre des responsabilités, ils peuvent seulement se résigner à faire quelque chose pour quelqu'un. Ils n'apprendront pas à prendre la responsabilité de leur propre vie.

Notre famille
J'ai trois enfants qui ont entre 13 et 21 ans. L'aîné a suivi pendant dix ans le cursus scolaire normal. Mon deuxième enfant la moitié de ce temps-là et mon troisième uniquement la première année. Je ne m'étais pas rendue compte jusque là que l'instruction en famille était une alternative possible dans certains cantons suisses.

Est-ce que je peux voir des différences entre mes enfants à partir du temps qu'ils ont passé à l'école ? C'est difficile à évaluer ! Les trois enfants sont de toute façon très différents. J'ai moins constaté de différences entre les trois enfants que de **changements** une fois qu'ils sont sortis de l'école. Tout particulièrement chez ma cadette, elle pleurait souvent, avait un très grand complexe d'infériorité et perdait vraiment espoir jusqu'à ce que je découvre qu'elle pouvait apprendre à sa manière à la maison. C'est aujourd'hui une personne bien équilibrée et volontaire. Je connais d'autres enfants qui ont commencé l'école à la maison plus jeunes, à qui ces opportunités ont été offertes plus tôt. Je trouve ces enfants encore plus épanouis. Ils ont les pieds sur terre. Ils reproduisent moins de comportements négatifs.

Comment nous faisons l'instruction à la maison – L'apprentissage informel et auto-géré
Je le fais tout simplement à ma manière. Je ne sais pas comment les autres font. Il existe en Suisse, différentes façons de faire l'instruction à la maison. Beaucoup le font pour des raisons religieuses ou alors ils font réellement " l'École à la maison " et enseignent. Voici un exemple typique de notre famille : Quand nous avons commencé l'instruction à la maison, mon plus jeune savait compter jusqu'à 20. Après les vacances d'été, sans qu'il ne se soit passé quoique ce soit de particulier durant cette période, il a pu soudain compter jusqu'à 100. Je pense qu'il a réussi cela essentiellement en utilisant de l'argent. Il s'intéressait à l'argent, le comptait, le classait, allait faire les courses et jouait avec mon porte-monnaie. Il faisait tout simplement des **expériences** avec l'argent. Naturellement, il ne veut pas se faire avoir lorsqu'il dépense de l'argent, ne pas payer trop cher et recevoir la monnaie exacte en retour.

Avec la lecture et l'écriture, c'est plus ou moins la même chose. Il y a de l'écrit partout et les nombres sont utilisés en permanence. Je suppose que dans une pièce noire où il n'y aurait rien à apprendre alors rien ne serait appris ou du moins aucun de ces savoirs de base. Mais à l'extérieur, dans la vie, où tous ces savoirs de base sont utilisés... De la même manière qu'ils apprennent à marcher, ils seront capables de lire et compter.

Le futur

Comment mes deux plus jeunes enfants s'en sortiront dans le monde du travail ? Pour ce qui est de mon fils, je vais devoir attendre et voir. Ma fille a un statut d'apprentie et elle est motivée pour réussir, en partie pour montrer aux autres qu'il est possible d'y arriver même sans diplômes officiels. Elle n'est pas particulièrement enthousiasmée par ma philosophie et ne saisit visiblement pas encore les avantages dont elle a profité. Je pense que ça lui a fait du bien ; elle est devenue si pleine de vie alors qu'elle manquait tellement d'assurance. Je sens qu'elle a maintenant les pieds bien sur terre et qu'elle réussira sa formation. Elle trouvera certainement son chemin dans la vie.

Bildung zu Hause in der Schweiz

Das Schweizerische Zivilgesetzbuch vom 10. Dezember 1907 verpflichtet die Eltern eines Kindes, für dessen Bildung und Erziehung inklusive seines körperlichen, geistigen und sittlichen Wohles zu sorgen. Die Gesetzgebung, welche die Bildung und Erziehung von Kindern in der Schweiz regelt, ist in jedem der 26 Kantone unterschiedlich. Die Durchsetzung der jeweiligen Gesetze erfolgt auf lokaler Ebene durch dort zuständige Entscheidungsträger (Marti Hanna, 1991, Enquete suisse sur le homeschooling, Endlich/enfin, No.2.). Einige Kantone stehen einer Bildung ohne Schulbesuch (Homeschooling, Homeeducation) aufgeschlossen gegenüber, in anderen Kantonen dagegen ist der Besuch einer staatlich anerkannten Schule Pflicht.

Eine ganze Reihe von Kantonen hat ihre Schulgesetze in den letzten Jahren geändert und die Regelungen, welche die Bildung eines Kindes in privater Initiative und zu Hause betreffen, verschärft. Diese Beschneidung des elterlichen Rechtes, die eigenen Kinder zu Hause in privater Initiative zu erziehen und individuell lernen zu lassen, verstösst möglicherweise gegen die Verfassung der Schweiz und weitere Bundesgesetze. Das müsste jedoch erst ausgelotet werden.

Bildung zu Hause ist noch immer ein recht ungewöhnlicher Lernweg für Kinder in der Schweiz. Kinder von Familien, die auf entlegenen Gehöften wohnen, Zirkuskinder und Kinder, deren Eltern anderen fahrenden Berufen nachgehen, erhalten in der Regel problemlos die Erlaubnis, zu Hause zu lernen. Das gilt im übrigen auch für Kinder aus internationalen Familien oder aus Familien, die nur vorübergehend in der Schweiz wohnen. Dagegen müssen sich schweizerische Familien wie auch alle anderen Familien, die ihren ständigen Aufenthalt in der Schweiz haben, um eine Genehmigung des häuslichen Lernens bemühen. Mitunter wird eine Darstellung dessen, was die Kinder zu Hause lernen, als Voraussetzung dafür verlangt. Beispielsweise kann die Aufstellung von Jahres- oder Wochenlehrplänen gefordert werden. Üblicherweise findet wenigstens einmal jährlich ein Besuch durch einen Vertreter der Schulbehörden statt.

Normalerweise müssen Kinder in einer der vier Landessprachen (Deutsch, Französisch, Italienisch oder Rätoromanisch) unterwiesen werden. Sofern ein Kind in einer beliebigen anderen Sprache unterwiesen werden soll, muss dafür eine Genehmigung eingeholt werden. Das Kind bleibt dennoch zum zusätzlichen Erlernen einer der vier Landessprachen verpflichtet. Normalerweise wird dies die Sprache des Kantons sein, in dem die Familie lebt.

Allen Hürden zum Trotz ist Bildung zu Hause eine wachsende Bewegung in der Schweiz. Die meisten Familien, deren Kinder zu Hause lernen, leben in den Kantonen Genf, Bern, und Zürich.

Lebensschulung zu Hause und selbstbestimmtes Lernen: Ein Beispiel aus der Schweiz

von Coni Lagler

Coni Lagler, Mutter von drei Kindern, berichtete uns aus der Schweiz. Sie sprach auf Deutsch.

Schulung zu Hause in der Schweiz

In der Schweiz haben wir einen Schullehrplan, der fast wie die Bibel gehandhabt wird. Wenn dann jemand die Kinder in der Weise wie ich zu Hause schult, ist das stets eine Art Gratwanderung, um mit den Behörden nicht in

Konflikt zu geraten und trotzdem seinen Kindern zu erlauben, sich in ihrer eigenen Weise zu entwickeln. Weil die Gesetze von Kanton zu Kanton unterschiedlich sind, ist es nicht überall möglich, die Kinder so zu begleiten.

Es gibt Kantone, wo so ein Familien-Projekt hätte aufgegeben werden müssen. In manchen Kantonen muss man ein ausgebildeter Lehrer sein, einem Lehrplan wie an der Schule folgen und Unterrichtsmaterialien benutzen. Im Kanton Zürich, wo ich lebe, wird es im Juni 2005 eine Volksabstimmung geben, die vielleicht die Schulung zu Hause für alle, ausser für ausgebildete Lehrer, unmöglich macht.

Ich kenne die Anzahl der Familien, die in der Schweiz zu Hause schulen, nicht. Im Kanton Zürich sind es rund 140 Familien. Ich weiss, dass einige von ihnen christlich ausgerichtet sind. Ich habe keinen Kontakt zu ihnen, weil wir verschiedene Lebensauffassungen haben.
In der Schweiz verstehen es viele nicht, wenn nicht die öffentliche Schule besucht wird. Es hängt von der Person ab, mit der ich spreche, aber gegenwärtig lasse ich mich selten auf eine Diskussion ein. Ich erkläre denen, die wirklich interessiert sind, was wir tun, wenn sie fragen. Ich behalte die Kinder aber nicht während der Schulstunden im Haus, um Fragen zu vermeiden. Es steht den Kindern frei, ob sie rausgehen oder nicht.

Wir haben eine etwas ungewöhnliche Situation, was den Kontakt mit den Behörden betrifft. Nach anderthalb Jahren, in denen wir Schulung zu Hause gemacht hatten, begann ich an einer Schule mitzuarbeiten, wo die Kinder in ähnlicher Weise behandelt wurden wie zuhause. Ich konnte die Kinder mitbringen. Deswegen liessen die Behörden mich für eine Weile in Ruhe. Die Schule, gegründet auf Ideen von Montessori und Rudolf Steiner, sollte sehr frei sein. Es funktionierte jedoch nicht. Die Erwachsenen konnten sich nicht einigen.

Die Schulpflegebehörde besucht Familien, die zu Hause schulen. Wir werden in der gleichen Weise kontrolliert, wie eine Schule kontrolliert wird, zweimal im Jahr. In meinem Fall verlief das relativ gut, aber nicht ganz ohne Schwierigkeiten. An manchen Orten kann man enorme Probleme erleben.

Normalerweise definiere ich meine Methode als eine 'erweiterte Montessori Philosophie'. Wir, die Kinder und ich, besprechen schon im Voraus, was sie während der zweistündigen Kontrolle (Inspektion) schreiben oder am

Computer arbeiten. So eine Art kleine Theaterinszenierung. Die Behörden würden es gerne sehen, dass wir Arbeiten vorzeigen um zu dokumentieren, was und wann es gemacht wurde. Bisher habe ich es geschafft, das zu umgehen.

Warum ich anfing, die Kinder selber zu Hause zu schulen
Für mich geht es vor allem darum, dass jedes Kind sich selbst sein kann. Jedes Kind lernt anders und jedes Kind hat unterschiedliche Interessen. Es ist wichtig für mich, dass Kinder voll Leben sind und dass sie mit sich selbst eins sein dürfen, dass sie ihr Selbstbewusstsein entwickeln können und nicht jemanden haben, der ihnen sagt, wie sie zu sein und was sie zu können haben. Kinder lernen laufen, wenn sie dafür bereit sind. Das ist der Weg, denke ich, wie alles Lernen geschieht.

Jeder ist ein Individuum und hat eigene Interessen, die zu entwickeln sind. Jeder hat seine eigenen Fähigkeiten und Stärken. Und ich denke, wenn jemand auf die Art lernt, die richtig für ihn ist, oder lernt, was auch immer für ihn stimmig ist, dann kann er *Verantwortung* dafür übernehmen. Wenn in der Schule gesagt wird: "Du mußt dieses und jenes machen, auf die Art, mit diesen Ergebnissen", dann sind die Kinder nicht fähig, Verantwortung zu übernehmen, sie können nur etwas für jemand anderen ausführen. Sie werden nicht lernen, Verantwortung für ihr eigenes Leben zu übernehmen.

Unsere Familie
Ich habe drei Kinder zwischen dreizehn und einundzwanzig Jahren. Das älteste besuchte zehn Jahre eine normale Schule. Mein zweites Kind zur Hälfte und mein drittes Kind nur das erste Jahr. Bis dahin hatte ich noch nicht herausgefunden, dass zu Hause schulen eine Alternative in einigen Schweizer Kantonen ist.

Kann ich Unterschiede zwischen den Kindern erkennen aufgrund dessen, wie lange sie zur Schule gegangen sind? Das ist schwierig zu erkennen! Alle drei sind sowieso unterschiedlich. Ich bemerkte weniger die Unterschiede zwischen den Kindern als die *Veränderungen*, als die Kinder nicht mehr in die öffentliche Schule gingen. Vor allem bei meiner mittleren Tochter, sie weinte oft, hatte einen massiven Minderwertigkeitskomplex und war richtig verzweifelt, bis ich herausfand, dass sie zu Hause auf ihre Art lernen konnte. Sie ist nun eine ausgeglichene und engagierte Person. Ich kenne andere Kinder, die auf dieselbe Weise von einem jüngeren Alter an zu Hause achtsam begleitet wurden, denen die gleichen Möglichkeiten früher gegeben wurden. Ich erlebe diese Kinder wesentlich offener, sie sind geerdeter und entwickeln weniger negative Verhaltensweisen.

Wie wir zu Hause fürs Leben schulen und lernen

Ich mache es einfach nach meiner Art. Ich weiss nicht, wie es andere machen. Es gibt in der Schweiz verschiedene Arten zu Hause zu schulen. Viele machen es aus religiösen Gründen, oder sie machen Schule zu Hause und unterrichten. Hier ist ein typisches Beispiel aus unserer Familie: Als wir mit der Lebensschulung anfingen, konnte mein Jüngster bis 20 zählen. Nach den Sommerferien, ohne abfragen oder ähnlichem, konnte er plötzlich bis 100 zählen. Ich glaube, das erreichte er vor allem durch den Gebrauch von Geld. Er fing an Geld zu kennen, zählte es, sortierte es, ging einkaufen und spielte mit meiner Geldbörse. Er machte einfach *Erfahrungen* mit Geld. Er will natürlich beim Geldausgeben nicht betrogen werden; er will nicht zuviel zahlen und er will das richtige Rückgeld bekommen.

Mit Lesen und Schreiben ist es ziemlich dasselbe. Es gibt ja soviel Geschriebenes überall, und Zahlen werden rundum benutzt. Ich nehme an, dass in einem dunklen Raum, wo es nichts zu Lernen gibt, auch nichts gelernt werden wird, zumindest keine von diesen Grundfähigkeiten. Aber draussen, im Leben, wo all diese Fähigkeiten benutzt werden... auf die selbe Art wie sie laufen lernten, werden sie fähig sein, zu lesen und zu rechnen.

Die Zunkunft

Wie meine zwei jüngeren Kinder wohl mit der Arbeitswelt zurechtkommen werden? Im Fall meines Sohnes muss ich abwarten und sehen. Meine Tochter hat einen Ausbildungsplatz und ist entschlossen, es zu schaffen, teilweise auch um anderen Leuten zu zeigen, dass es auch ohne offizielle Schulabschlüsse gehen kann. Sie ist nicht besonders begeistert von meiner Philosophie und begreift vermutlich noch nicht die Vorteile, die sie davon hatte. Ich glaube, es tat ihr gut, sie ist so lebensvoll geworden, obwohl sie so unsicher war. Ich fühle, dass sie nun mit beiden Füssen fest auf dem Boden steht und dass sie die Ausbildung schaffen wird. Sie wird sicher ihren Lebensweg finden.

Useful Addresses/Adresses utiles/ Nützliche Adressen

Education Otherwise
PO Box 325, Kings Lynn,PE34 3XW, UK
Tel: 0870 7300074   www.education-otherwise.org

Hes Fes
PO Box 20284, London NW1 3WY, UK
Tel: 0044 (0)207388 0559   www.hesfes.co.uk

Les Enfants d'Abord
Secrétariat , La Croix St Fiacre ,F-03110 Vendat, France
Tel: +33 3 (0)8 70 36 42 44   www.lesenfantdabord.org

Bundesverband Natürlich Lernen! e.V. (BVNL)
Anke Caspar-Jürgens, Lange Straße 10,D-17440 Klein Jasedow;
Tel.: +49 (0) 38374 – 75256   www.bvnl.de
Christiane Ludwig-Wolf, Im Wäsele 2,D-72525 Trailfingen
Tel.: +49 (0) 7381 – 3960
www.homeschooling.de
www.leben-ohne-schule.de
www.menschenskinder2000.de
www.netzwerk-bildungsfreiheit.de

Bildung zu Hause
Bildung zu Hause Schweiz ,Postfach 1996,CH-8401 Winterthur, Schweiz
www.bildungzuhause.ch

Learning Unlimited
1 Croxley Road, London W9 3HH, UK   www.learning-unlimited.org

European Forum for Freedom in Education
Husemannplatz 3-4, D-44878 Bochum, Deutschland   Tel: +49 234 6104736
www.effe-eu.org